New Each Day

New Each Day
A Spiritual Practice for Reading Psalms

Rabbi Debra J. Robbins

FOREWORD BY
Rabbi Andrea L. Weiss, PhD

CCAR
Press

REFORM JUDAISM PUBLISHING
A DIVISION OF CCAR PRESS
CENTRAL CONFERENCE OF AMERICAN RABBIS
5784 NEW YORK 2024

Published by Reform Judaism Publishing, a division of CCAR Press
355 Lexington Avenue, New York, NY 10017
(212) 972-3636 | info@ccarpress.org | www.ccarpress.org

Library of Congress Cataloging-in-Publication Data

Library of Congress Cataloging-in-Publication Data
Names: Robbins, Debra J., 1963–author.
Title: New each day: a spiritual practice for reading Psalms / Rabbi Debra J.
Robbins; foreword by Rabbi Andrea L. Weiss, PhD.
Description: New York, NY: Central Conference of American Rabbis, CCAR Press,
[2024] | Includes index.
| Summary: "Jewish liturgy includes a psalm recited to mark each day of the week.
The book offers insights on each psalm, with a structure for meditation and writing
to encourage the reader to develop their own routine. The book also includes reflec-
tions for each month, based on the psalm recited for Rosh Chodesh"—Provided by
publisher.
Identifiers: LCCN 2023016909 (print) | LCCN 2023016910 (ebook) | ISBN
   9780881236415 (trade paperback) | ISBN 9780881236422 (ebook)
Subjects: LCSH: Bible. Psalms—Meditations.
Classification: LCC BS1430.4 .R63 2023 (print) | LCC BS1430.4 (ebook) |
   DDC 223/.206--dc23/eng/20230526
LC record available at https://lccn.loc.gov/2023016909
LC ebook record available at https://lccn.loc.gov/2023016910

Interior design and composition by
Scott-Martin Kosofsky at The Philidor Company, Rhinebeck, NY
Printed in U.S.A.

10 9 8 7 6 5 4 3 2 1 0

הַמְּאִירָה לָאָרֶץ וְלַדָּרִים עָלֶיהָ
בְּרַחֲמִים וּבְטוּבָה
מְחַדֶּשֶׁת בְּכָל־יוֹם תָּמִיד
m'chadeshet b'chol yom tamid
מַעֲשֵׂה בְרֵאשִׁית:

The Illuminator lights up the world
and all of her inhabitants with mercy,
and in Her goodness,
each day renews
the act of creation.

—YOTZEIR OR, *from the morning liturgy;*
translation by Rabbi Josh Warshawsky

In gratitude for all the ways that Rabbi Debra Robbins nurtures our congregation, Temple Emanu-El of Dallas, Texas, through her remarkable gifts of heart and spirit.

Joni and Bob Cohan
Julie and David Fields
Nina Cortell and Dr. Bob Fine
Sarah C. and Michael J. Fisher
Alissa and Bobby Goodman
Betsy and Mark Kleinman
Allan and Barbara Kogan
Leslie and Bob Krakow
Stephen and Jane Saginaw Lerer
Susan C. Longo
Rita Paresky
Jody and Dr. Mel Platt
Helen and Frank Risch
Louise and David Rosenfield
Michelle and Mike Sims
Phyllis and Ron Steinhart
Robin Kosberg and Rabbi Mark Washofsky
Tina and Richard Wasserman

Contents

Foreword

Rabbi Andrea L. Weiss, PhD

THE SAGES OF OLD bequeathed to us a week's work of psalms to recite day in and day out. In *New Each Day: A Spiritual Practice for Reading Psalms*, Rabbi Debra J. Robbins provides a disciplined, deeply rewarding way to access these ancient texts. Attuned to the potential power of each word and the satisfaction of maintaining a daily spiritual practice, Rabbi Robbins encourages us to follow her example: find a special spot, read the assigned psalm with intention, and reflect on what it means for you on that very day, on each new day.

Rabbi Robbins speculates as to why the Rabbis may have enshrined Psalms 24, 48, 82, 94:1–95:3, 81, 93, and 92 as the seven daily psalms. I will admit that these are not the psalms I would have selected to read week after week, year after year. A few might have made my list—maybe Psalm 82 or Psalm 92—augmented by others that I find more resonant or more artfully constructed, like Psalms 8, 13, 30, 90, and 126. But in the end, the reasons the Rabbis chose these psalms do not really matter.

According to Rabbi Robbins, what matters is that we have inherited this list and the liturgical tradition of reading a different psalm each day of the week, the *Shir Shel Yom* (Psalm of the Day). She insists that each word of these psalms contains hidden secrets, unique to each of us, if we but pause in practice and pay attention to hints of meaning in each psalm. She models an atomized mode of reading, an associative mode of reading, an accessible mode of reading that believes that even the most obscure words or concepts—even the most beguiling verses—contain potential meaning if we but linger and look for links to our contemporary lives.

In *New Each Day* and her earlier book, *Opening Your Heart with Psalm 27*, Rabbi Debra J. Robbins invites us to develop a daily practice of reading and writing about the psalms that have been extracted from their scriptural home in the Book of Psalms—or *Sefer T'hillim* (The Book of Praise) in Hebrew—and incorporated into the prayer book. Through this process, we become acquainted with this biblical book—also called the Psalter—an anthology of ancient poems written by unknown and largely unidentified authors over the course of several hundred years, likely prior to the start of the second century BCE.

The daily psalms, like the 150 compositions in the Psalter, can be grouped into several main genres. Hymns or Psalms of Praise (like Psalms 92, 95, and 104) celebrate God's awe-inspiring qualities and beneficent deeds. Psalms of Lament (like Psalms 13 and 94) contain the impassioned pleas of individuals or communities in crisis. Psalms of Thanksgiving (like Psalms 30 and 138) tell of past distress while testifying, with gratitude and wonder, to God's responsiveness. Some psalms provide historical retrospectives on Israel's past (like Psalms 81 and 105) or offer wisdom about how to live a virtuous life and avoid the ways of the wicked (like Psalms 1 and 24). Others have been labeled as subgenres such as Zion Songs (Psalm 48) and Enthronement Psalms (Psalm 93), or they resist easy classification (like Psalm 82).

Throughout these different genres, we find formulaic language and repeated structural patterns. For example, many psalms mention enemies, be they literal or figurative (e.g., Psalm 94:3). In laments, no matter how dire the situation, cries to God for help usually give way to expressions of confidence in God's saving powers (e.g., Psalm 94:22–23). Hymns often contain second-person plural commands as the psalmists call on others to raise their voices or instruments in praise of God, most famously phrased as *Hal'lu Yah* ("praise *Yah*/God," as seen in the first and last words of Psalms 146–150). The psalms envision God with an array of metaphors, the most prominent in the daily psalms being the depictions of God as a protective rock or fortress (e.g., Psalms 48:4, 94:22) and as a powerful king who rules with justice and some-times with vengeance (e.g., Psalms 24:7–10, 93:1, 94:1–2). These seven psalms, like others in the Psalter, marvel at Creation (e.g., Psalms 8:4, 24:2), look longingly to Jerusalem (e.g., Psalms 48, 137), and imagine rivers and other natural forces joining the chorus of divine praise (e.g., Psalms 93:3, 98:8).

Because of their artistry and imagination, and because they give voice to timeless, universal experiences and emotions, people in countless lands and languages have recited psalms for thousands of years. Still today, psalms continue to give voice to what it means to be a human being and to what it means to be part of the people Israel bound in a covenantal relationship with our God. Theologian Rabbi Rachel R. Adler, PhD, encapsulates what makes these ancient compositions so compelling when she writes, "The book of Psalms is the record of a truthful relationship between embodied, fragile humans who inhabit an unpredictable world and a God who is intermittently present and sometimes terrifyingly absent to its inhabitants."[1]

By invitation and by example, Rabbi Debra J. Robbins shows us how to read the daily psalms and make them meaningful for us week after week. Recite a blessing, delve into the day's psalm, pick up a pencil, take a breath. See what you can discover about the psalms and about yourself through a regular, disciplined practice of *Shir Shel Yom*.

Rabbi Andrea L. Weiss, PhD, is Jack, Joseph and Morton Mandel Provost and associate professor of Bible at the Hebrew Union College-Jewish Institute of Religion. She organized the 2017 and 2021 "American Values, Religious Voices" campaigns and coedited *American Values, Religious Voices: 100 Days, 100 Letters* (Vol. 1), and *American Values, Religious Voices: Letters of Hope from People of Faith* (Vol. 2). She served as the associate editor of *The Torah: A Women's Commentary* (CCAR Press, 2008), is the author of *Figurative Language in Biblical Prose Narrative: Metaphor in the Book of Samuel*, and has written many articles on metaphor, biblical poetry, and biblical conceptions of God.

Invitation and Introduction

I DON'T KNOW if the great modern Hebrew Israeli poet Lea Goldberg had a spiritual practice of reading a biblical psalm each day. In one of her poems, she sings like the Psalmist, "Teach my lips . . . a hymn of praise . . . lest routine set my ways,"[1] suggesting that even this inspired writer of poems needed a source to give voice to the world she saw around her in early twentieth-century Palestine. It was a world filled with the diverse beauty of fruit trees, the decay of leaves at the turn of the season, the injustices of war, poverty, and suffering of neighbors, yearning for hope and peace. She turned her personal observations and universal feelings into poems, much like the ancient psalmists did, echoing their language in her hymn of praise, as her blessing, to the Holy One who renews our days.

Drawing on the description of a biblical ritual described in the Mishnah, around the second to third century of the Common Era, Jewish tradition developed the custom of *Shir Shel Yom* (Psalm of the Day), adding a cycle of seven psalms, biblical liturgical poem/songs, to the daily morning liturgy. The rabbis who selected and placed these psalms may or may not have been Lea Goldberg's teachers, but they certainly have been mine. Reading a different hymn of praise each day helps ensure that we don't see the new day as the one before. The seven-day cycle propels us forward, inviting us to notice the bright beauty of creation and the darkness that shrouds human systems of justice. This routine allows us to look into ourselves and beyond ourselves—to see others as vulnerable regardless of how vulnerable we may feel—in the community that needs us.

I like routines and have learned from Lea Goldberg that the best ones should not be too routine and completely set our ways. The cycle of *Shir Shel Yom* offers the ideal balanced practice: the psalms remain constant, but the person reading them and the surrounding world are new each day, making it impossible for "routine to set our ways." It is always Psalm 24 on Sunday, 48 on Monday, 82 on Tuesday, followed by

94 on Wednesday and then 81 on Thursday. Friday is assigned Psalm 93, and the week culminates on Shabbat/Saturday with Psalm 92. The psalms identified two thousand years ago have amazingly remained the same, but what has not endured beyond the briefest of explanations of the choices is the answer to the question "Why these seven psalms?" I'll share six possibilities, confident that you, the reader, will provide a seventh as a result of engaging in this practice.

- With 150 psalms to choose from, why not start with Psalm 1 and just keep reading one a day for 150 days and then begin again? A cycle of 150 doesn't match anything in the natural cycle of Creation, but a cycle of seven matches God's days of Creation from the Torah and the human creation of the "week" to reflect it.
- Some of the psalms are very long—Psalm 119 has 176 verses— and others are short— Psalm 117 has plenty of power packed into its two verses. The *Shir Shel Yom* package of seven is well-balanced: the shortest selection is five verses (Psalm 93 for Friday) and the longest only twenty-six (Psalms 94:1–95:3 for Wednesday).
- The content of the 150 psalms is as diverse as human emotions and experiences, and the seven selected are well curated to reflect the possibilities and trajectory of daily and weekly life, keeping the focus on arriving at Shabbat.
- Certainly in biblical times, and at least until Johannes Gutenberg began to print Bibles in 1454, very few individuals owned their own books or could read; in contrast, the singing of psalms— biblical poems set to music—was accessible to all. Mastering a repertoire of seven, in addition to some of the others for special occasions, was a manageable lifetime achievement.
- Another option might have been to allow each person to select their own seven psalms. This (at least for me) is daunting, and I'd likely spend my lifetime simply trying to choose rather than engaging in the practice.
- Most compelling is the connection that comes with the practice. These seven may not be my favorite psalms, but they are the treasures and traditions of my ancestors, like the pearls I wear that belonged to my great-aunt or the recipes I make from my

grandmother's cards on Passover. I feel connected across time to all the generations before me who have offered the same poems—in different languages and using different translations—for more than two thousand years. I feel connected with others in my generation whom I will never know, but with whom I am in relationship as we share the same practice, engaging with the same text every day.

I have come to love these psalms and the steady flow from week to week that comes with their practice. On this Monday I am not the same as I was the Monday before, and the light is not the same and the temperature is not the same; events in the world, in my life, have all shifted in ways large and small. And a Tuesday in November, between Election Day and Thanksgiving, is not the same as the Tuesday in January after Martin Luther King Day, or in August during the Hebrew month of Elul, when our time to prepare for the High Holy Days draws near. Each week and each month is different, but *Shir Shel Yom* anchors us and gives us a secure mooring as our lips learn, over and over again, to offer blessing.

New rituals can help keep the routines from becoming "too routine," especially when they are grounded in the ancient practices of our people and the texts of our tradition. The *Shir Shel Yom* practice of this book is an outgrowth of the Psalm 27 practice developed in *Opening Your Heart with Psalm 27*, in response to those who practiced with me for seven weeks and then found themselves without a daily psalm routine to set their way. New to the traditional practice of reading psalms is the integration of a second traditional practice of marking the arrival of each Hebrew month. Grounded in biblical history, Jewish rituals have evolved to mark the onset of the new Hebrew month, Rosh Chodesh, indicated when the moon appears as a slim crescent. The month grows as the moon does, with the full moon marking the fifteenth day, and then wanes toward its conclusion after twenty-nine or thirty days.[2]

For women in particular, Rosh Chodesh came to be associated with an additional day of rest, a pause, given as a reward for their embrace of sacred ritual.[3] A big grand psalm, a hymn to Creation and so much more, Psalm 104 was selected for monthly reading as the new moon appeared in the sky.⁴ This practice of *Shir Shel Yom*, crafted for *New Each Day*, embraces Rosh Chodesh as an opportunity to pause in the weekly psalms cycle, to turn to Psalm 104 and reflect on how its words prepare us to bless and praise in the month ahead and further help us keep even the routine of reading *Shir Shel Yom* from becoming too fixed as a practice and thereby setting our ways, keeping us from change and growth and insight.

The seven psalms of *Shir Shel Yom* have a shared vocabulary of essential Hebrew words that speak to the enduring values and beliefs of Jewish life. It can be nearly impossible to notice this when reading a translation, as each is an act of interpretation and commentary by the translator. But familiarity with a few basic words and their possible translations can unify the seven psalms in a way that might otherwise go undetected. This is why it can be very helpful to use multiple translations when exploring any biblical text.

The Babylonian Talmud permits us to recite the *Sh'ma* in any language we can hear (which the Rabbis interpret to mean "understand").⁵ And we can deduce that if it was permissible for this most essential prayer, it would also be permissible for other prayers and biblical texts, like Psalms. So reading *Shir Shel Yom* in a familiar language is important for this practice. And at the same time, it's important to remember that Hebrew is an extraordinary language. The same alphabetical root system used in the Bible and by the Psalmist provides the structure and building blocks for the Modern Hebrew language spoken by Israelis today, thanks to the foresight and gifts of Eliezer Ben-Yehuda.⁶ It's a small language compared to some others, but being compact allows the texts from various times and places to resonate in the ear and mind. Stories and songs bump into each other in our imaginations as the meaning of the words becomes at once more precise and more expansive.

Psalm 24, the psalm for Sunday—in Jewish time, the first day of the week—introduces the essential vocabulary with six key Hebrew words, each of which appears at least once later in the week. To highlight these essential words, sometimes this book capitalizes the Hebrew root letters in transliteration (more details can be found on page xxxii). *DoR*, "generation," connects us to Monday in Psalm 48. *TZeDeK*, "righteousness," is a theme of Psalm 82 on Tuesday. *NeFeSH*, "human breath," the essence of soul, grounds us on Wednesday, being used twice in Psalm 94. *LeV*, "heart," is at the center of Psalm 81 on Thursday. Friday's Psalm 93 echoes back to Sunday with the word *KaDoSH*, "holiness." And finally, the word *OLaM*, meaning "world" and "eternity," binds the mundane week with the enduring holiness of Shabbat in Psalm 92.

There are other essential words that appear throughout the week. *Chesed*, "loving generosity," appears three times, and *mishpat*, "justice," appears in four of the psalms. The familiar word from our prayer service, *sh'ma*, "to listen or hear," is used four times, and the word *tzur*, "rock," is used to describe God in three of the seven psalms. I don't think the Rabbis of antiquity chose these psalms because of these linguistic connections, but I certainly find the shared language helps to unify the journey from day to day.

As a teaching tool, the collection of seven provides a wonderful introduction to a Psalms curriculum. There are varied ways that the 150 psalms begin, with attribution to the supposed author, King David, or with notes to a musical leader; some seem to be a dedicatory introduction, and others begin as an announcement, a cue to the congregation: this is a song, get ready to sing. The seven selected for *Shir Shel Yom* each begin in a different way, making use of five common headings, as well as two examples that open with an urgency to begin the day and its work.

The psalms are also arranged in an order that helps to organize the way we can approach the flow of the week. We move gently from Shabbat into the week on Sunday, with nourishing imagery of the world God created. Monday presents us with a litany of verbs to get us acting and caring all week long. On Tuesday, the reality of the week sets in, and we begin to confront the enduring challenges of our broken world. Wednesday is the darkest, when we are called to stand for justice, which is not easy for us or for our Creator. On Thursday, we begin to turn toward Shabbat—we are invited to sing, and we taste a bite of the sweet words that will welcome the day of rest. Friday's psalm is the shortest, as if to save ourselves for the abundance of psalms that will fill the most sacred of days.[7] On Shabbat, we arrive at Psalm 92, its opening verse proclaiming its place: "a song of Shabbat." And then, rested and refreshed, we begin again.

The Baal Shem Tov (1698–1760, Ukraine) understood the importance of reading psalms daily, weekly, and monthly throughout one's life. He and his students lived in a world that was often dark and challenging. They sought continually to find sparks of God's light—holiness in the world around them—in every blade of grass, in every human face, in the deepest depths of despair, and in each word of sacred Scripture. The Baal Shem Tov taught, "Everyone has a psalm in the Book of Psalms, to be read each year, according to their age. If a person is twelve, Psalm 13 should be read."[8] This practice is similar to *Shir Shel Yom* in that it offers a single text to illuminate the world for a year followed by an opportunity to grow into another, with fresh themes and images as we continue to bless and praise.

We use these psalms, each on its appointed day, as

- Gateways to language, learning, and a way of life that sustains.
- Tools to organize our social, emotional, political, and spiritual lives.
- Prompts to praise in a world where we often forget to be grateful.
- Affirmations that we are human and have the capacity—unlike all the creatures of the earth and all the angels of the heavens—to open our hearts and mouths to offer blessing and praise.

The Talmud expresses our role beautifully in this fanciful teaching:

People are more dear to the Holy One than the ministering angels,
as humans may recite a song of praise to God at any time,
but ministering angels recite a song of praise only one time per day.
Some say that the ministering angels recite a song of praise one time
  per week.
And some say that they recite a song of praise one time per month.
And some say that they recite a song of praise one time per year.
And some say that they recite a song of praise once every seven years.
And some say that they recite a song of praise one time per Jubilee
  [every fifty years].
And some say that they recite a song of praise one time in the entire
  history of the world. (Babylonian Talmud, *Chulin* 91b)[9]

But not us. So, let's begin with a blessing, a hymn of praise, a psalm that will be new each day.

Historical Background of *Shir Shel Yom*

The ritual of offering psalms daily begins in the Bible. I Chronicles 16:5–6 preserves the names of the musicians who performed this sacred task along with their various instruments. The text uses the same word for the offering of psalms in the Temple—*tamid*—as for kindling the oil lamp of the *Mishkan*, the desert Tabernacle, during the forty years of wandering in the wilderness.[10] The light was tended *tamid*, "regularly," to ensure that it, like God's presence, would never be extinguished. So too, the words of psalms become regular, constant reminders of that presence, not only in communal and public practice, but in our personal lives.

What the I Chronicles text does not include is the specific words that were used to invoke God's name, praise God's Creation, and extol the powers of *Adonai*. The void is filled by following generations with creative ideas, some of which are rejected in subsequent generations and some of which endure. By the time of Rabbi Akiva (one of the most renowned and respected first-century Rabbis living after the destruction of the Second Temple in Jerusalem), seven biblical psalms had been identified, one for each day of the week. This established the *tamid*, the regular practice, of *Shir Shel Yom*, the daily psalm.

In the Mishnah, the Rabbis describe an elaborate ritual that they imagine took place around the sacrificial offerings, with the sounding of the shofar and the recitation of a different psalm each day, which they divided into three sections.[11] They then identify the psalm assigned to each day. Reading their text is a little tricky, because it was written before chapters and verses were assigned to the Bible and the Rabbis quote only the opening line of the psalm to identify it! The Mishnah does not tell us why or how each psalm was chosen, if there is an overarching theme to the psalms, if combined they identify an arc of action for the week. (I'd really like to know about the debates that likely took place and which psalms were not chosen for each day!) The text carefully lays out each day and the opening verse of its assigned psalm, with no comment until the seventh day, Shabbat. Psalm 92 is identified and then the passage concludes, "[This is] a psalm, a song for the future, for the day that will be entirely Shabbat and rest for everlasting life."[12]

As Jewish life continued to thrive in the face of tremendous challenge, greater detail and explanation were needed for the commandments of the Torah and the early practices of the Mishnah to be observed in widespread and diverse Jewish communities. The Talmud helped unify Jewish ritual and ethical values across the Diaspora.[13] In one Talmudic passage, the prolific Rabbi Y'hudah (135–170 CE) teaches about the Psalm of the Day.[14] To give weight to his opinion, he cites it in the name of Rabbi Akiva, who lived at the time of the Mishnah (c. 50–135 CE). The earlier practice of reciting the Psalm of the Day in three sections accompanied by shofar blasts does not stand the test of time, but the selection of the specific psalms does. Rabbi Y'hudah tries to make sense of the weekly trajectory by superimposing it on the seven days of Creation, stretching his imagination (and ours too) to make them match. Like many rituals, this one was likely widely practiced and the selections well established, memorized, and perhaps beloved, so they became standardized in the daily and Shabbat liturgical structures that were evolving.[15] The practice endures as *Shir Shel Yom* guides the way for modern mortals to witness the world's changes: season to season, month to month, renewing itself year after year, new each day.

The seven psalms identified in the Mishnah and discussed in the Talmud took hold and became part of the liturgical canon. As prayer books developed, customs around cycles of the year, the months, the week, and the day took hold in various ways around the Jewish world. Eventually Eliyahu ben Shlomo Zalman (the Vilna Gaon, 1720–97) offered a new explanation of the seven psalms based on a teaching from the *Zohar*.[16]

This interpretation imagines Jewish history divided into seven 1,000-year segments.[17] Sunday's psalm (Psalm 24) spans from Creation to the Flood. Monday represents the biblical period featuring Mount Moriah. On Tuesday, the Torah is given at Sinai. Wednesday alludes to the one thousand years surrounding the destruction of the Temple. On Thursday, Judaism survives for one thousand years without the Temple (we should not be surprised that the Rabbis identify themselves and the writing of the *Zohar* in this period). The sixth historical period has yet to begin (at least in my opinion). It will be a time when humanity will unite and recognize that God is once again all-powerful, ruling over all of Creation. The final thousand years will be characterized by the best qualities of Shabbat, a messianic era of renewal and justice, of joy and peace. Again, the proof texts may be a bit of a stretch, but the invitation to travel through history over the span of each week is stimulating on an intellectual level and motivating as a spiritual approach.

In the twenty-first century, a variety of prayer books include the practice of *Shir Shel Yom*, adding the recitation of the Psalm of the Day to the morning liturgy after the *Aleinu* prayer and before the Mourner's *Kaddish*. Rabbi Jonathan Sacks (1948–2020) writes in his commentary to the *Koren Siddur*, "A special psalm was said in the Temple on each of the seven days of the week. We say them still, in memory of those days and in hope of future restoration [of the Temple, its sacrificial rituals and priestly leadership]."[18] For those, like me, who may not aspire to a restoration of the ancient sacrificial systems and exclusively inherited male leadership, Rabbi Hershel Matt (1922–87) in the daily siddur of the Reconstructionist Movement explains the practice and trajectory of psalms as reflecting the social and political realities of our contemporary world: "The seven psalms culminate in the psalm for the Sabbath day. The week begins and ends in harmony but in the middle, we are exposed to a world of terrible suffering. . . . Shabbat is the day of true vision, on which all the contradictions of everyday existence are resolved."[19]

In Reform Judaism, we are encouraged to educate ourselves about various religious or spiritual practices and then determine for ourselves what will be most meaningful. *Shir Shel Yom* are not included in our daily siddur, and as a result, we have the opportunity to experience them in their original places, within the Book of Psalms. This is an invitation to draw upon the history, traditions, and original language of the psalms to find new ways of giving voice to these seven hymns of praise.

Historical Background of Psalm 104 for Rosh Chodesh

Psalm 104 is grand in its description of God's power and presence: majestic in its imagery of all Creation, authentic in its assessment of our feelings and failures, demanding in its expectations of humans—to work, to hope, and to praise. The words sing of God's work, creating moon and sun, each with a place and time to shine, part of the planetary balance of the universe from the very beginning, and of humanity's small place in that vast cosmos.

The Rabbis saw the arrival of the new moon as a great promise. They ascribed to this perpetual and eventually predictable natural wonder the greatest hope of the Jewish people: that we and our world would be continually renewed like the moon and thus endure forever. In shaping the celebratory blessing for the new moon, they turn to the culminating verses of Isaiah's prophecy, "For as the new heavens and the new earth that I am making stand before Me, said *Adonai*, so shall stand your seed and your name. And it shall be, from one month to the next and one sabbath to the next, all humanity shall come to bow before Me, said *Adonai*."[20] The Rabbis also include in this blessing one verse from Psalm 104, "God made the moon to mark the seasons; the sun knows when to set."[21] A post-Talmudic source documents the integration of this pair of verses into a special blessing over wine offered on Rosh Chodesh sanctifying the new month. [22] Later sources suggest that the entire psalm was offered at the start of the month by the Levites.[23] In time, Psalm 104 came to be included in both the Ashkenazic and Sephardic prayer books, immediately following the daily psalm, *Shir Shel Yom*. For the practice of *Shir Shel Yom*, the recitation of Psalm 104 punctuates the difference between the Psalms of the Day and the beginning of each month, introducing themes and images to forecast and frame the daily work for the coming month.

The sliver of the moon and its accompanying long psalm are reassurance of our small place in the universe, God's infinite creative capacity, the spiritual work that lies before us, the hope that endures, and the gratitude we can offer even in the darkness. In harmony with the ancient Psalmist, we affirm, "I will offer psalms to *Adonai* as long as I live; with all my being I will sing praise to God."[24]

Get Started

The specifics of this spiritual practice were developed to use with Psalm 27 over a seven-week period surrounding the Jewish High Holy Days and shared in Opening Your Heart with Psalm 27. *Thanks to the input of many students and the insight that can come with experience, some elements have been adapted or enhanced, while others remain as anchors for the daily work of reading psalms.*

Learn to Read

The practice of *Shir Shel Yom* is an invitation to relearn how to read. Reading a psalm every day is different from reading the newspaper or email every day. It is not even quite the same as reading a daily passage of Scripture. The ancient biblical poems are like letters between lovers—expressions from the heart set down in verse, about a day, the world, the other lover. They capture human emotions of dark fear, deep longing, rage, and doubt, and of course abundant joy, sheer awe, and overflowing gratitude.

Love letters are read slowly in private, with as few distractions as possible, often over and over again. This allows a phrase or image—maybe a single word—to rest in the reader's heart and imagination. Reading a psalm every day in this way means trying to concentrate and savor one bite of the poem, rather than feeling obligated or responsible for consuming the whole Psalm of the Day at one sitting. This *Shir Shel Yom* practice of reading, with its partners of writing and reflection, takes about twenty minutes, and when divided into the five-minute sections described below, it becomes accessible and manageable.

Many people have an initial reaction to reading the same material over and over again and wonder, "Won't it get boring?" For some it might, but the repetition of reading a psalm, like reciting a poem or singing a song, often allows, as Elliott Holt reflects, "the lines on the page to release their music and their meaning. Repetition cultivates a deeper kind of attention, one that pushes past facile understanding to intimacy with the work."²⁵ The practice of *Shir Shel Yom* holds out that promise and more. Because the poems/songs/psalms (the word in Hebrew, *t'hillim*, is the same for all three) partake of the sacred, encountering them on the page every day is an opportunity for intimacy with the Holy One and with those made in the image of the Holy One (other people). Holt articulates the aspiration of our work: "This practice of sustained concentration can also nurture human connection by encouraging intimacy of attention. Maybe we can learn to read one another the way we read poetry, listening closely to the music we all make."²⁶

Shir Shel Yom creates space for "daily devotional" in Jewish life. It's reading one psalm, one verse, one phrase—maybe only one word—every day, all year. You can do this work on your own, as part of a small group, or with a partner; it works beautifully both online and in person. *Shir Shel Yom* is accessible in any setting, anywhere, anytime, on any day.

- It might supplement another spiritual practice you already have.
- It might become a new ritual or sacred habit.
- It might lead you to a bigger awareness—about yourself, about Judaism—or to more learning and blessing.
- It might even change your life, your ideas about God, sacred Scripture, or prayer, your soul, your heart.

It will change your day and make it new.

Start to Write

Susan Cain introduced me to John Pennebaker's work studying people who write down what flows not only from the head but from the heart. In his research he found that "people who wrote about their troubles were markedly calmer and happier than those who wrote about their sneakers . . . and physically healthier. . . . 'Expressive Writing,' where our feelings and experiences make their way, honest and raw, onto the page can help us learn to live with insight, especially if we do it regularly."²⁷ According to John Steinbeck, "In writing, habit seems to be a much stronger force than either willpower or inspiration."²⁸ For writers, like athletes and musicians, not only habit but ritual helps them succeed at their work. While these rituals may seem to be quirky or repetitive, the routine is often transformed into a spiritual practice. Just as we can train the muscles of the hand to write, ritual trains the muscles of the heart to reflect, to create, and to connect with emotions, experiences, memories, hope, ourselves, and yes, God. This book is a way to begin the training.

For me, it helps to write longhand in a bound composition book on a fresh page each day. I find it satisfying to see the pages fill up, the wide lines and size of the paper make it less overwhelming to think about filling the page with words, and it's a deterrent from tearing out pages. Date each page and write the title of the Reflection for Focus at the top, or write the whole verse if you prefer. Copying the words is a powerful way to encounter the language. I recommend you try to resist the impulse to write on a computer, tablet, or phone, because writing electronically is how we build spreadsheets, text our friends, post to social media, conduct business. This is a different kind of work and requires a different tool, so if you can, consider trying a different modality to create a mindset and practice. You may discover you are less likely to self-censor and edit and instead allow the words to flow onto the page. I write in pencil. Shakespeare wrote in ink, as did the psalmists. Many contemporary authors who write longhand, like Natalie Goldberg, prefer pen, as it flows quickly. For me, pencil lead is slow enough on the page to move in sync with my brain, and it doesn't fade with time like ink. Naomi Shihab Nye says it perfectly:

> There will not be a test.
> It does not have to be
> a Number 2 pencil.
> But there will be certain things—
> the quiet flush of waves,
> ripe scent of fish,
> smooth ripple of the wind's second name—
> that prefer to be written about
> in pencil.
> It gives them more room
> to move around.[29]

Either way, with pencil or pen, on the computer or on paper, commit to yourself: no erasing, no crossing out, no judging. Just keep writing. Let the words, whatever they are, fill the paper (or the screen), and you can be confident, they will be new, each day.

Build a Routine

Following the practice of my writing coach from more than twenty-five years ago, with an endorsement from John Grisham, I try to write in the same place, at the same time, every day. This builds muscle memory. "Ah yes," my body says, "I sit in this chair, at this table, facing this window, this wall, in this room, and I know what to do here." The light is different, the temperature is different, the material, the Psalm of the Day and Reflection for Focus are both different. I am different today, but this time and this place are the same, and I know what to do here: I write. I also need a clear uncluttered space in which to write, to limit my distractions (which I highly recommend even if you think all the stuff doesn't bother you). Billy Collins says it perfectly in his poem "Advice to Writers":

> Clean the space as if the Pope were on his way.
> Spotlessness is the niece of inspiration . . .

I'm not expecting the pope but am hopeful that I might encounter something holy—maybe God's presence will alight on the desk or wrap itself around me or inspire me for just an instant in these five minutes. And so, I prepare to experience Collins's words:

> . . . you will behold in the light of dawn
> the immaculate altar of your desk,
> a clean surface in the middle of a clean world.[30]

What better way to welcome God's presence, to encourage it to join me, for even an instant of inspiration.

Forgive

In the cycle of the Jewish year, it can feel like forgiveness is reserved for one season (the seven weeks surrounding Yom Kippur, the Day of Atonement), but repentance is meant to be part of daily life. Rabbi Eliezer teaches in the Talmud, "Repent today, lest you die tomorrow,"[31] meaning each day should include *t'shuvah*, seeking forgiveness. The daily prayer service prompts us, "Forgive us. . . . Blessed are You, *Adonai*, abounding in forgiveness."[32] If God is abounding in forgiveness, shouldn't we, made in God's image, be forgiving as well? And shouldn't we be as willing to forgive ourselves as we are others? This is especially important in taking on the practice of *Shir Shel Yom*. This work requires that you forgive yourself every day. Here's how it may go:

You'll say, "I didn't write much in five minutes."
Respond, "Forgiven."
You'll say, "I couldn't stay focused when I sat still."
Respond, "I forgive myself."
You'll say, "I totally forgot to practice today."
Respond, "I'm forgiven."
And over and over again you'll say, "Try again."
   "Try again." "Try again."
Respond, "I will."

It's what *t'shuvah* is all about. I missed the mark. I'll regather my materials. I'll try again tomorrow. Back at the desk, pencil in hand, timer set. When I fall out of the practice, I'll try again tomorrow. I'll try every day, for one month and then the next, for the whole year, psalm by psalm and phrase by phrase, each one a step toward a year of wholeness and holiness.

Be Grateful

Rabbi Pinchas, Rabbi Levi, and Rabbi Yochanan agreed, and taught in the name of Rabbi Menachem of Galya, that ultimately what matters most in our lives and our world is expressing gratitude. They all shared a love for elaborate rituals and bringing their life experiences to interpreting sacred texts, yet they imagined a time where it would vanish and all that would remain would be words of thanks, songs of praise, and poems of gratitude to God—The Holy One We Call by Many Names and Know in Infinite Ways.[33] Their well-reasoned analysis leads them to conclude there will not be a single formula for giving thanks; instead there will be infinite forms of expression offered an uncountable number of times. *Shir Shel Yom* invites us, as we conclude our practice every day, to take to heart the words of Psalm 100, *Mizmor L'Todah*, to offer a Psalm of Thanks. The practice closes with a few words of gratitude—for having spent time in a sacred space where our mouths flow with praise, and we give voice with the ancient words *Hodu lo, bar'chu sh'mo!* "Give thanks to *Adonai*, praise God's name!"[34]

Notes to Readers

The Jewish Calendar and Rosh Chodesh

The Jewish calendar is structured on both the cycle of the sun and the orbit of the moon; it offers structure to the day, each week, every month, and the entire cycle of a year. Days in Jewish life begin at night (based on the passages in Genesis 1 "there was evening and there was morning"); the week concludes with Shabbat and begins with Sunday (reflecting the Genesis 2 texts of God's work being complete on the seventh day). Months follow the cycle of the moon, beginning when the moon is new and concluding when the moon is no longer visible to the human eye. The monthly calendar is adjusted seven times over nineteen years to keep the Jewish holidays in their appropriate seasons (at least in the Land of Israel, if not the Southern Hemisphere). This adjustment is made in the spring with the addition of a second month of Adar. For the *Shir Shel Yom* practice, it is recommended to use either the Adar Reflection for Focus a second time or the Reflection for Focus for the specific day.

The Jewish calendar has several days referred to as "new years." According to the Mishnah,[35] there are four cycles that continue to organize the year for Jews: the first of Elul is the new year for animals; the first of Tishrei (Rosh HaShanah) is the new year for the world; the fifteenth of Sh'vat (Tu BiSh'vat) is the new year for trees; the first of Nisan—the month during which we celebrate Pesach—is the first month of the calendar year. With so many opportunities to start a new year, your *Shir Shel Yom* practice can begin in any month, on any day, and continue through the annual cycle until it begins again. It is customary from the beginning of Elul through the celebration of Simchat Torah to read not only the Psalm of the Day but also Psalm 27 (*Opening Your Heart with Psalm 27* is a guide to that practice). Alternatively, *Shir Shel Yom* practice allows for the flexibility to switch to Psalm 27 for that seven-week period and then return to the monthly cycle of Psalm of the Day. It is recommended that on each Rosh Chodesh, the designated monthly

Reflection for Focus be used in place of the daily one; when there is a second day of Rosh Chodesh, I suggest returning to the Daily Reflection for Focus. There are multiple additions and adjustments to the traditional practice of reading psalms as part of holy day celebrations and ritual practices; details are available in various siddurim. A ten-year calendar with the corresponding dates of the Hebrew months can be found on page 159, and the CCAR Luach App is an excellent and accurate source for the dates as well.

The Structure

The book is divided into three separate sections. The first section introduces each psalm in the *Shir Shel Yom* cycle with a Reflection for Focus that looks at the psalm in its entirety. This section is meant solely as an introduction. You can read these Reflections for Focus as often as you like, though they were not designed to be part of the monthly cycle. The second section guides you through an entire month by selecting four phrases from each of the seven *Shir Shel Yom* psalms and exploring them through Reflections for Focus, resulting in four for each day of the week. This section is designed to be visited again, and again, and again. The third section offers a Reflection for Focus for each month, designed to be read at Rosh Chodesh using Psalm 104. Each Reflection for Focus is resonant with the month or season of the year. They appear in order of the Hebrew months rather than the order of the psalms. The index includes the verses explored in each psalm of all three sections.

Hebrew and Translation

The Hebrew of the Psalmist has become the Modern Hebrew language, spoken in the twenty-first century. The vocabulary is built on a system of root letters that can be constructed differently to convey gender, tenses, contexts, or related meanings. Even if you don't (yet!) read Hebrew, this practice is an opportunity to see connections between words in the printed letters that may not be apparent in a poetic translation. You can easily identify the Hebrew root letters of some transliterated words because the root letters are capitalized; for example, *kadosh* becomes *KaDoSH* to indicate the core letters associated with holiness (page 84 has a great example of this approach). I relied on Rabbi Richard Levy's elegant *Songs Ascending: The Book of Psalms*.[36] I love it, as I hope you will, and I encourage you to read other translations, as each offers a unique interpretation of the ancient words. A list of suggestions is included in "Resources for Reading Psalms."

Notes

Many of the Reflections for Focus are built around an additional biblical verse, a Jewish text, or a secular source that may pique your interest in Jewish study. To limit the distractions on the page, the notes for the Reflections for Focus, as well as sources for the translation of Hebrew words, are found at the back of the book and identified by phrase. Certain exceptions have been made when the content of the note deepens the context of the Reflection for Focus. The notes for the introductory prose sections can be referenced on pages 143–45.

Music

Music is an important element of spiritual practice, and I am grateful to my dear friend Cantor Richard Cohn for showing me how each moment has a melody to accompany it. Cantor Cohn has composed seven short *nigunim*, accessible melodies without words, one for each day of the week to accompany us through the week and add a layer of commentary to each psalm. You can read more about their composition in the Composer's Commentary beginning on page xxxv. The composition is called *Nigunei Shir Shel Yom*, and is accessible on the CCAR Press website. We recommend using the melody written for Psalm of the Day to begin your daily practice and hope you will find, as we have, the notes remain with you as a reminder of the sacred work.

Names for God

This book offers a variety of metaphors and names to express the infinite ways of encountering the Divine and avoids the use of gendered pronouns to refer to God. I most often address God as *Adonai* (Ah-doe-nigh, the vocalization of the ineffable Hebrew letters spelling one of God's names, *yod, hei, vav, hei*). Despite the fact that this name translates into English literally as "my Lord," I use this name because it is, for me, the most familiar form of address for God from the prayer book and the Bible. I embrace *Adonai* as an accessible, authentic, and neutral name for the Holy One. I invite you to use names for God that speak to you, perhaps in a new way, each day.

Composer's Commentary

Cantor Richard Cohn

WHEN RABBI ROBBINS began to develop this inspiring practice of engagement with each of the daily psalms in its cyclical context from week to week, we wondered what kind of musical practice might align well with the *Shir Shel Yom*. We decided to explore the possibility of a *nigun* for each day—that is, an orienting melody for Sunday, Monday, and each day of the rest of the week through Shabbat and beginning again the next Sunday. We now have seven *nigunim*, which you will find on the CCAR Press website and can download for personal use. (On Rosh Chodesh, we recommend utilizing the melody designated for whatever day of the week it may be.) Our hope is that returning to soon-to-be-familiar melodies again and again in their rotational sequence will help ground your overall practice with both a sense of regularity and an opportunity for new discoveries over time, analogous to the process of study and investigation Rabbi Robbins has set forward for the psalm texts themselves.

The *nigunim* are not crafted to interpret the psalms according to their meaning or literary context. Rather—mirroring the days of the week—the *nigunim* form a sevenfold cycle in which each bears its own identity while contributing to the evolution of the entire group. Underlying this structure is a metrical progression based on a primary pulse for each *nigun* beginning with Sunday ("in 1"), moving to Monday ("in 2"), and continuing all the way to Shabbat ("in 7"), reflected in the time signatures found in the written score. This mathematical architecture is, however, *not* the main point, and you may experience other metrical divisions or formulations within and across the musical suite that vary from the one-through-seven concept. The melodies are deliberately brief so as to aid memorization and to facilitate the virtue of repetition—that is, taking a mantra-like approach to the practice of singing the melodies as many times as you'd like during a given day's practice.

The *nigunim* should not be experienced as static. You are invited to sing them at differing tempos and volumes, with greater or lesser sense of smoothness or impulse. It is also possible to change the vowels or other sounds for singing, although at first you may wish to follow the recommended cycle (from humming on Sunday to "oo" on Monday and so forth), to see how the rotation of vowels from day to day informs your practice, solidifies associations with specific days, and helps to organize the week.

Various musical micro-motifs circulate among the seven *nigunim* and do some shape-shifting along the way, perhaps creating some inner coherence among the evolving forms. The first three melodies already have built-in variations with which you can experiment. Beginning with Wednesday's melody, located at the central pivot point in the week (four of seven), you are on your own for any adaptations! The *nigun* for Thursday begins to incline toward the feeling-direction of Shabbat, and by Friday you may notice a stepping down of propulsive energy in preparation for the Day of Rest. The *nigun* for Shabbat itself has a melodic quality that oscillates between major- and minor-tonality points of inflection, emulating an aspect of Ashkenazic chant that manifests the Sabbath as existing in an ephemeral realm not limited or contained by any single scalar or harmonic form. The seventh *nigun* is sung to the words "*Shabbat shalom*," but you are welcome to sing it wordlessly if you prefer. The *nigunim* are not harmonized, to provide for maximum flexibility in how they express themselves.

Ultimately, the seven *nigunim* are offered as a scaffolding for your own practice, the meaning or significance of which will emerge organically from the unique associations you create with them in your singing from day to day and week to week. Enjoy!

Tools for the Practice

The practice can more easily become a sacred routine if you have everything you need ready and you learn how to navigate the psalms and
Reflections for Focus in the book, so each one is new each day. It helps
to have the following:

1. A notebook (or computer if you must) and a pencil (or pen).
2. A timer (the one on a phone is fine if you can silence everything
   else).
3. Your copy of this book (you may want an additional translation
   of Psalms).
4. The ten-year calendar on page 159, to find the day the Hebrew
   month begins.
5. A download of *Nigunei Shir Shel Yom*, the seven *nigunim* (musical
   interpretations) composed by Cantor Richard Cohn, to begin
   your practice each day. These can be found on the CCAR Press
   website.

The daily practice is always the same. The details are outlined, along
with proposed timing, in "Daily Directions" on page xl.

The words of poet Wendell Berry express the practice perfectly in a
single paragraph. In his poem "How to Be a Poet (to remind myself),"
he imagines the amazing possibilities that can come from sitting still
and doing this work every day:

> *Accept what comes from silence.*
> *Make the best you can of it.*
> *Of the little words that come*
> *out of the silence, like prayers*
> *prayed back to the one who prays,*
> *make a poem that does not disturb*
> *the silence from which it came.*[1]

Our experiences teach us that so much can come from silence. The words of the psalms likely came to the Psalmist from silence. Wendell Berry's poem—like the poems of Lea Goldberg, Billy Collins, and Naomi Shahib Nye—sing like a prayer that comes from silence. And the same can happen for us—little words, new each day, waiting for us to accept them—from our silence.

A challenge of this practice is navigating the calendar—trying to keep track of the day of the week, the week of the month, when the new Hebrew month begins, and when something special is happening in the Jewish year that adjusts the reading of psalms, not to mention finding the right page for the right Psalm of the Day and its accompanying Reflection for Focus. You will surely find your own system (maybe colored sticky notes or bookmarks) for the monthly and annual cycles, and "Guide for the Month" on the next page may be helpful as you get started. The page numbers for the Rosh Chodesh Reflections for Focus are included in "Guide for the Month," as well.

Guide for the Month

Psalm of the Day
The Reflections for Focus cycle begins again at the start of each Hebrew month, after pausing for the Rosh Chodesh readings.

Rosh Chodesh (Start of the New Hebrew Month) Reflections for Focus
The secular dates for Rosh Chodesh can be found in the Appendix and on the CCAR Luach app, as well as other electronic or print Jewish calendars.

Daily Directions

Get Settled

- Gather your notebook, pencil, and timer.
- Locate the pages for the Psalm of the Day and the Reflection for Focus in *New Each Day*.
- Sit still, pay attention, take a deep breath.
- Listen to, hum along with, or even sing one of the *nigunim* (wordless melodies).
- Read the blessing, inserting the appropriate words from the list provided.
- Take another deep breath.

Read

- Read the Psalm of the Day in English (ideally aloud) or in Hebrew if you can.
- Read the Reflection for Focus.

Write

- Set the timer for five minutes and start it.
- Write whatever comes to mind about the Reflection for Focus or something you noticed about a word, phrase, or idea in the psalm. It doesn't matter what you write—just write. Don't edit or erase, and try not to censor your words; just write for just five minutes.
- Use one of these prompts if you need help getting started:
  How does this phrase in this psalm speak to me today?
  What memories or images, aspirations or questions does this psalm evoke?

Sit

- Set and start the timer for five minutes, again.
- Sit comfortably. Your feet might be on the floor, hands could rest on your lap or thighs, and perhaps close your eyes or lower your gaze.
- Try to pay attention only to your breath moving in and out of your lungs.
- Then, try to think about the phrase related to the Reflection for Focus, or what you just wrote, or what you just read. When you get distracted, go back to paying attention to your breath, and try again to think about what you read or wrote, or say the phrase over and over in your head.

Wrap It Up

Write out these three short sentences, or at least reflect on them:

- To show compassion for yourself:
    I forgive myself for . . .
- To allow the psalm to stay with you:
    I want to remember . . .
- To give thanks for making time for this sacred practice:
    I am grateful . . .

New Each Day

Yom (Day) יוֹם	Day of Week	Number
Yom Echad יוֹם אֶחָד	Sunday	first
Yom Sheini יוֹם שֵׁנִי	Monday	second
Yom Sh'lishi יוֹם שְׁלִישִׁי	Tuesday	third
Yom R'vi-i יוֹם רְבִיעִי	Wednesday	fourth
Yom Chamishi יוֹם חֲמִישִׁי	Thursday	fifth
Yom Shishi יוֹם שִׁשִׁי	Friday	sixth
Yom Shabbat יוֹם שַׁבָּת	Saturday	seventh

Chodesh (Month) חֹדֶשׁ

Tishrei	תִּשְׁרֵי
Cheshvan	חֶשְׁוָן
Kislev	כִּסְלֵו
Tevet	טֵבֵת
Sh'vat	שְׁבָט
Adar	אֲדָר
Adar Rishon אֲדָר רִאשׁוֹן	
Adar Sheini אֲדָר שֵׁנִי	
Nisan	נִיסָן
Iyar	אִיָּר
Sivan	סִיוָן
Tamuz	תַּמּוּז
Av	אָב
Elul	אֱלוּל

Shir Shel Yom Blessing

הִנְנִי מוּכָן וּמְזֻמָּן \ מוּכָנָה וּמְזוּמֶּנֶת \ מוּכָנֶה וּמְזֻמֶּנֶה

Hin'ni muchan um'zuman/muchanah um'zumenet/muchaneh um'zumeneh...

male   female   nonbinary

Here. Now. I am present and prepared.
I am ready to join my voice
to the sacred songs of the universe
with the daily practice of the past:

לְהַזְכִּיר וּלְהוֹדוֹת וּלְהַלֵּל

l'hazkir, ulhodot, ulhaleil

to remember,
and to thank,
and to praise,
with each psalm on its day.

הַיּוֹם ____ בְּשַׁבָּת, לְחֹדֶשׁ ____.

חֹדֶשׁ   יוֹם

Hayom ____ b'Shabbat, l'chodesh ____.

yom (day)   *chodesh* (month)

Today is ____ the ____ day of the week, in the month of ____.

day of week   number   month

בָּרוּךְ יְיָ אֱלֹהֵי יִשְׂרָאֵל מִן־הָעוֹלָם וְעַד הָעֹלָם ... אָמֵן.
וְהַלֵּל לַיְיָ.

Baruch Adonai, Elohei Yisrael, min ha-olam v'ad ha-olam ... Amen.
V'halel l'Adonai.
I bless You, Adonai, God of Generations, from eternity to
eternity ... Amen.
And, hallelu-Yah.

Introductions
to the
Shir Shel Yom
Psalms

Introduction to Sunday, Psalm 24
The text for Psalm 24 is on page 22.

The Dawn of Creation.
The Beginning of It All.
Psalm 24: The Way to Start Each Week.
Order and openings, internal and eternal gates,
always in God's presence.
A seven-day spiritual curriculum,
a core vocabulary for conversation,
as ancient poems speak with each other and us,
and days unfurl toward Shabbat.
The language of lovers,
or of siblings, understood in silence,
by unseen bonds of holy connection.

Sunday, refreshed by Shabbat, we are *DOR DORshav*,
a generation of generations.
Monday, confident celebrators of God's presence,
we speak the stories of wonder and gratitude
l'DOR acharon, we are inspirations for future generations.

Sunday we aspire to manifest *TZeDaKah*,
God's redemptive justice.
Tuesday, advocates and agents of the Judge,
we see the poor and suffering,
haTZDiKu, we rise for fairness and justice for all.

Sunday, souls rested, we notice, *NaFSHi*,
breath sustains our lives.
Wednesday, each breath becomes a reminder,
the soothing gift of the soul
shachnah dumah NaFSHi
y'shaashu NaFSHi
we give thanks for its nourishing, nurturing power.

Sunday with pure heart, *bar LeiVaV*,
we stand in God's presence.
Thursday, like Pharaoh with *sh'rirut LiBam*, stubborn hearted,
we listen to song and shofar sound
and rise from the Egypts, the narrow places, to nourishment.

Sunday offers gateways to honesty, justice,
free entry into *makom KaDoSH*, a holy place.
Friday, the work yet incomplete,
we anticipate the celebration,
the blessing to sit,
surrounded by *naavah KoDeSH*, beautiful holiness.

Sunday sets the schedule,
a singular focus in ten verses,
Adonai, God,
everywhere,
all the time,
in everything.

Sunday speaks the language of life,
the mountain of work for the week,
God's challenge looms large.
Rested and re-souled,
we return to the week, to the words,
tall and strong, noble,
with hope,
this week,
our labor will bear fruit,
for God's world,
in God's presence.

Introduction to Monday, Psalm 48

The text for Psalm 48 is on page 24.

Monday is a busy day.
But first, as a friend says,
"Always begin with gratitude and the rest will come."
And so, this day dawns as the psalm begins:
Thank You, Great God—
for this beautiful world You made
in which I dwell,
Hallelujah!

On this day, as every day,
terror and trembling await.
Ears attune to the laughter of love
and sweet words of Torah,
and to hear the human cries of pain.
Eyes open to the beauty of a blooming flower,
and the kindness of one toward another,
and to so much that needs repair in Your world.
With a breath of creation, coming from the east,
I meditate on God's *chesed*,
and my own striving for it.
God's hand filled with justice,
and the injustice of our streets and courts.

I want to despair but am called by my sisters to rejoice.
Inspired by them I turn to the day.
Six verbs in two verses,
So much to do before
the psalm ends,
the day concludes.

סֹבּוּ *Sobu*. Walk.
Go around and around, again and again.
Take it all in, from every angle,
be prepared for anything.

וְהַקִּיפוּהָ *V'hakifuha*. Embrace.
Extended arms in a big wide circle.
Hold close what is most precious:
myself, my loves, God's world.

סִפְרוּ *Sifru*. Count.
Number not only buildings, but blessings.
Each a vantage point to consider
what's gone before, what's yet to come,
all worthy of praise.

שִׁיתוּ *Shitu*. Set the Heart.
Declare an intention, a direction.
Recommit, again, to overcome battlements, impediments,
of body, mind, and spirit.

פַּסְּגוּ *Pasgu*. Scale the Heights.
Climb in the mind, with the imagination.
Glimpse possibilities of hope and healing and even peace,
everything seems possible on a Monday.

תְסַפְּרוּ *T'sapru*. Recall the Story.
Before the day comes to an end, tell its story.
A busy day, a long one, a lonely or difficult moment,
each memory shared is a gift for generations to come.

Remember, this is a day that God has made,
rejoice to be alive on it.
Give thanks to God for the Mondays,
throughout all time and space.

Introduction to Tuesday, Psalm 82

The text for Psalm 82 is on page 28.

It's Tuesday.
Sweet tastes, beautiful melodies, sacred connections,
the *oneg*, the joy, of Shabbat
is a memory.
I am as far from last Shabbat
as I am from next Shabbat,
in the middle of the mundane,
the work of the week,
the raw realities of a fractured world.
It's hard to hear *Havdalah*'s plea
to Elijah, to each of us:
Please, bring healing and peace,
quickly, now, before it's too late.

It's Tuesday and it's the day to read Psalm 82,
a timeless choice, dating back to the Mishnah.
Written in an ancient world that looks so modern,
gritty and grimy, battered and broken.

It's not Sunday
with Psalm 24's invitation to ascend God's mountain
n'ki chapayim uvar leivav,
with clean hands and pure hearts.

It's not Monday
with Psalm 48's majestic views of a Jerusalem not yet realized,
tageilnah b'not Y'hudah,
women rejoicing and dancing in celebration of justice.

It's not Wednesday
with Psalms 94–95's anticipation
of gathering for Shabbat,
L'chu n'ran'nah l'Adonai,
Come, let's sing thanks to God.

It's not Thursday
with Psalm 81's reminder of our story,
Joseph and Miriam calling us to account,
tiku vachodesh shofar,
listen, not once a year, but each month, each week, each day.

It's not Friday with Psalm 93's painting,
The Vastness of God's Eternal Presence,
balanced, in harmony,
l'orech yamim,
forever and a day.

It's Tuesday,
and today we read Psalm 82.
The audacious voice,
aggressive in its call,
to God and to us:
Uvnei Elyon kulchem,
Children of the Most High
stand up, like Abraham, for justice, for all,
every Tuesday, every day.

Introduction to Wednesday, Psalms 94:1–95:3

The text for Psalms 94:1–95:3 is on page 30.

Today we meet
God of Vengeances.
On Wednesday we greet
God Who Redeems from Egypt.

The Holy One of Exodus,
sends plagues as punishments,
hurls horses, chariots, and human beings into the sea.
We recoil at the Sacred,
Royal rage unleashed,
Majestic might,
cruelty crushing the souls of the innocent.
We try to resist this divine quality in ourselves,
and like God,
we fail.

On Wednesday we petition,
God Who Is the Judge of the Earth,
Rise.
Take a stand against arrogance, evil, iniquity,
make them pay, punish them,
wipe them away with your Power.
And then, we realize,
we are they.
We are the fools who fail
to use our eyes to see, our ears to hear.

On Wednesday we hear the warning.
On the fourth day of Creation,
the God of Genesis
formed the sun, moon, and stars,

set the cycles of the universe,
taught them to rotate and spin, balance and use gravity.
Beware of the false idols of celestial beauty,
and the earthbound ones too:
power, popularity, perfection.
They are not gods.

On Wednesday our God is
God of Many Names,
each one part of the Wholeness of Holiness:
God of Jacob
Teacher of Human Beings to Know
My Help
Soother of My Soul
Fortress
My Rock of My Refuge
Listener to Our Song.

On Wednesday
when the day ends,
walk with thanks
in the ever-present Presence of
God.

Introduction to Thursday, Psalm 81

The text for Psalm 81 is on page 34.

When the week is long with burdens:
loads of laundry or buckets of responsibility,
baskets and boxes of anxiety, fear, and pain,
the weight of loneliness
(it's amazing how heavy something so singular can be),
on Thursday, read Psalm 81.

When the days are short in minutes:
scarce daylight due to season or storm,
misplaced priorities or misunderstood projects,
or hours that flew fast with deep love, new learning, simple joy,
on Thursday, read Psalm 81.

On the day before Friday,
the day before the day before Shabbat,
when it's not too late to realize, recognize, remember,
or maybe even regret—
when it's already almost the end of the week—
read Psalm 81 as prelude and preparation,
for the day when burdens lighten, and time expands.

Thursday is a day to sing.
Sing to celebrate this day, sing an old song, sing any song,
prepare to sing a new song, soon.
Tune the instruments—strings and horns and drums,
attune the human voice with the Breath of God,
anticipate the harmony of being One.

Thursday is a day to tell a story.
We went out of Egypt.
We are always going out of Egypt.
We are always moving,
from narrow spaces to the wide openings of the wilderness,
toward new freedoms and responsibilities.

Thursday is a day to practice listening.
Hear the creatures of earth and sky,
created on this fifth day when the world was new.
Hear the voices of people who love me
and those who need my love.
Prove the Psalmist wrong,
I can, I will, listen to God's voice,
walk in God's ways.

Read Psalm 81 on Thursday
and savor
again, and again
and again,
the taste of honey that comes from the Rock,
our Rock and our Redeemer,
a sweet gift from God to fill our open mouths,
our open hearts, our open minds
as we make our way, together,
forever, and ever.

Introduction to Friday, Psalm 93

The text for Psalm 93 is on page 38.

Thank God.
Thank God for blessing someone with inspiration. And then,
thank the Rabbis of the Babylonian Talmud,
in tractate *Rosh HaShanah* on page 31a,
for selecting Psalm 93 as the psalm to read on Friday.
Thank the Rabbis of generations past,
for choosing a psalm with very few words.
Perhaps they understood, these lovers of language,
that today, less is more.

Maybe they said . . .
On Friday let's not overwhelm them with words.

Let's leave space (and time)
for the flow of psalms that will welcome the Sabbath bride.

Let's give just a taste,
so they will desire more of this sweetness.

Let's give them just a hint of how the words will:
come like waves one after another after another,
roll in from a distant time and place,
thunder with their voices,
splash onto their lives and soak into their hearts,
reveal God's power and presence.

Psalm 93 is packed with action for Friday.
The tottering world of the week
comes to a close.
Shabbat will be a time of re-souling
but this day-before demands energy,
alacrity of body and mind.

The five verses help us prepare
to rest from our work of creation,
to remember our Exodus from Egypt.
Robe in nobility.
(Clothes don't matter, godlike actions and attitudes do.)
Set a table (rather than a throne)
with a flower, a friend, a book, a prayer.

Be humble.
The most powerful waves are not more powerful than God,
and neither are we.
Notice God's beauty.
Holiness around us and within us,
sea, sun, sand,
a beating heart,
the flow of breath.
Leap.
Move big and fast.
Shabbat can't wait, we need it in our lives,
now.

Thank God.
Thank the Rabbis.
Now, thank yourself for reading Psalm 93 on Friday.

Introduction to Shabbat/Saturday, Psalm 92

The text for Psalm 92 is on page 40.

Maybe it was an obvious choice.
One asked: *What psalm should be sung on Shabbat?*
One answered: *Psalm 92—*
it's the only one of one hundred and fifty
to begin, "a song of the Day of Shabbat."

Or maybe it was a historical choice.
The biblical narrative recalls,
Levites sang praise songs to God in Jerusalem.
The Talmud affirms Rabbi Akiva taught his students
to sing Psalm 92.

Maybe the choice was more considered.
In anticipation of Shabbat,
double portions of wilderness manna fall at dawn on Fridays.
A second soul glows within, on Shabbat.
A psalm giving thanks to God, sung, twice.
In the evening,
tell of God's faith in us,
and ours in each other,
alongside friends.
In the morning,
tell of loving connections,
to God and all of Creation,
in a chorus of gratitude.

And then, there are the sevens.
On the seventh day, the crowning day of Creation,
God's tiniest name, *Adonai,*
spelled with the smallest of letters,
yod yod,
hides seven times in sixteen verses.
Take away the heading and there are fifteen.

Two sets of seven
(each a symbol of fullness and completion),
linked by high praise for our Creator,
"You are on high forever, *Adonai*!"

Or maybe it was the hope.
Psalm 92 was an easy choice,
a vision of what our world could be.
A taste
to inspire us,
to celebrate and care for all Creation,
to sustain the world
with justice and righteousness for all,
to pause from petition to praise.
A time
to imagine ourselves and our world,
strong, solid, steady,
enduring like the Rock.
Cracks
and
shattered
bits
are made
whole
once again,
and no imperfection is found.

שִׁיר מִזְמוֹר לִבְנֵי־קֹרַח: גָּדוֹל יְיָ וּמְהֻלָּל מְאֹד בְּעִיר אֱלֹהֵינוּ הַר־קָדְשׁוֹ: יְפֵה נוֹף מְשׂוֹשׂ כָּל־הָאָרֶץ

Shir Shel Yom Psalms

Psalm 24 for Sunday

1 Of David: A song.

To God belongs the earth and its fullness,
The world, and those who dwell within it.
2 For You founded it upon the seas,
You established it upon great rivers.

3 Who shall ascend to the mountain of Adonai
And who shall stand at Your sacred site?

4 Clean hands shall, and an honest heart;
One who raises up no falsehood to deface
  My name;
Who has not sworn an oath that hides deceit—
5 This one shall raise up a blessing from Adonai
And justice from the God of our deliverance.
6 This is the seed of seekers after You,
These are the ones who look for Your presence,
This is Jacob—selah!

7 Raise up your heads, O regal gates—
Let yourselves be raised up, O doors to eternity!
Let there enter the Ruler of Glory!
  8 Who is this Ruler of Glory?
Adonai, strong and mighty;
Adonai, mighty in battle!

9 So raise up your heads, O regal gates—
Raise up the doors to eternity!
Let there enter the Ruler of Glory!
  10 Who is this, this Ruler of Glory?
ADONAI OF HOSTS!
This is the Ruler of Glory—selah!

תהילים פרק 24

1 לְדָוִד מִזְמוֹר

לַיְיָ הָאָרֶץ וּמְלוֹאָהּ
תֵּבֵל וְיֹשְׁבֵי בָהּ׃
2 כִּי־הוּא עַל־יַמִּים יְסָדָהּ
וְעַל־נְהָרוֹת יְכוֹנְנֶהָ׃

3 מִי־יַעֲלֶה בְהַר־יְיָ
וּמִי־יָקוּם בִּמְקוֹם קָדְשׁוֹ׃
4 נְקִי כַפַּיִם וּבַר־לֵבָב
אֲשֶׁר | לֹא־נָשָׂא לַשָּׁוְא נַפְשִׁי
וְלֹא נִשְׁבַּע לְמִרְמָה׃
5 יִשָּׂא בְרָכָה מֵאֵת יְיָ
וּצְדָקָה מֵאֱלֹהֵי יִשְׁעוֹ׃
6 זֶה דּוֹר דֹּרְשָׁיו
מְבַקְשֵׁי פָנֶיךָ יַעֲקֹב סֶלָה׃

7 שְׂאוּ שְׁעָרִים | רָאשֵׁיכֶם
וְהִנָּשְׂאוּ פִּתְחֵי עוֹלָם
וְיָבוֹא מֶלֶךְ הַכָּבוֹד׃
8 מִי זֶה מֶלֶךְ הַכָּבוֹד
יְיָ עִזּוּז וְגִבּוֹר
יְיָ גִּבּוֹר מִלְחָמָה׃

9 שְׂאוּ שְׁעָרִים | רָאשֵׁיכֶם
וּשְׂאוּ פִּתְחֵי עוֹלָם
וְיָבֹא מֶלֶךְ הַכָּבוֹד׃
10 מִי הוּא זֶה מֶלֶךְ הַכָּבוֹד
יְיָ צְבָאוֹת הוּא מֶלֶךְ הַכָּבוֹד סֶלָה׃

Psalm 48 for Monday

1 A song, a psalm of the sons of Korach.

2 Great is Adonai, and greatly praised.
In the city of God, the holy mountain—
3 A beautiful height, source of rejoicing for all
    the earth,
Mount Zion, the expanses of the North—
Town of the mighty monarch.
4 Amid her palaces reigns God,
Well known as an impregnable fortress.

5 For behold the rulers assembled,
They marched across together,
6 They saw, indeed they were amazed—
They rushed to and fro in terror!
7 Trembling seized them there,
Writhing like a woman giving birth.
8 With but a wind sent from the east
You smash the ships of Tarshish.

9 As we have not shut our ears, so we have not
    shut our eyes,
In the city of Adonai of hosts, in the city of
    our God,
God has established it forever—selah!
10 We have meditated on Your covenantal love
In the innermost parts of Your Temple.

11 Like Your name, God, so is Your praise, to
    the ends of the earth;
Your right hand is filled with justice.

12 Let Mount Zion rejoice,
Let the daughters of Judah be glad
Because of Your judgments.

תהילים פרק 48

1 שִׁיר מִזְמוֹר לִבְנֵי־קֹרַח:

2 גָּדוֹל יְיָ וּמְהֻלָּל מְאֹד
בְּעִיר אֱלֹהֵינוּ הַר־קָדְשׁוֹ:

3 יְפֵה נוֹף מְשׂוֹשׂ כָּל־הָאָרֶץ
הַר־צִיּוֹן יַרְכְּתֵי צָפוֹן
קִרְיַת מֶלֶךְ רָב:

4 אֱלֹהִים בְּאַרְמְנוֹתֶיהָ
נוֹדַע לְמִשְׂגָּב:

5 כִּי־הִנֵּה הַמְּלָכִים נוֹעֲדוּ
עָבְרוּ יַחְדָּו:

6 הֵמָּה רָאוּ כֵּן תָּמָהוּ
נִבְהֲלוּ נֶחְפָּזוּ:

7 רְעָדָה אֲחָזָתַם שָׁם
חִיל כַּיּוֹלֵדָה:

8 בְּרוּחַ קָדִים
תְּשַׁבֵּר אֳנִיּוֹת תַּרְשִׁישׁ:

9 כַּאֲשֶׁר שָׁמַעְנוּ | כֵּן רָאִינוּ
בְּעִיר־יְיָ צְבָאוֹת בְּעִיר אֱלֹהֵינוּ
אֱלֹהִים יְכוֹנְנֶהָ עַד־עוֹלָם סֶלָה:

10 דִּמִּינוּ אֱלֹהִים חַסְדֶּךָ
בְּקֶרֶב הֵיכָלֶךָ:

11 כְּשִׁמְךָ אֱלֹהִים כֵּן תְּהִלָּתְךָ
עַל־קַצְוֵי־אֶרֶץ
צֶדֶק מָלְאָה יְמִינֶךָ:

12 יִשְׂמַח | הַר־צִיּוֹן
תָּגֵלְנָה בְּנוֹת יְהוּדָה
לְמַעַן מִשְׁפָּטֶיךָ:

13 Walk around Zion, encircle her,
Count her towers,
14 Set your heart on her battlement,
Walk among her palaces—
That you may tell tales of them to the next
   generation.
15 For this God is our God throughout all time
   and space;
God will lead us *al mut.*

¹³ סֹבּוּ צִיּוֹן וְהַקִּיפוּהָ

סִפְרוּ מִגְדָּלֶיהָ:

¹⁴ שִׁיתוּ לִבְּכֶם | לְחֵילָה

פַּסְּגוּ אַרְמְנוֹתֶיהָ

לְמַעַן תְּסַפְּרוּ לְדוֹר אַחֲרוֹן:

¹⁵ כִּי זֶה | אֱלֹהִים אֱלֹהֵינוּ עוֹלָם וָעֶד

הוּא יְנַהֲגֵנוּ עַל־מוּת:

Psalm 82 for Tuesday

1 A psalm of Asaph.

God stands up in a godly congregation,
Passing judgment in the midst of godlike judges:

2 "How long will you judge unjustly,
Raising up the face of the wicked—selah!
3 Judge righteously lowly and orphan,
Vindicate the afflicted and the poor!
4 Liberate the lowly and the needy,
From the hand of the wicked, deliver!

5 "They do not know, they do not understand
In deep darkness they stumble to and fro—
All the foundations of the earth are tottering!
6 I, God, have said: You are godlike beings,
And all of you are children of the Most High.
7 Surely, like any human beings, you will die
And like any one of the princes, you will fall."

8 Arise, God, judge the earth
For You will possess all the nations.

תהילים פרק 82

1 מִזְמוֹר לְאָסָף

אֱלֹהִים נִצָּב בַּעֲדַת־אֵל
בְּקֶרֶב אֱלֹהִים יִשְׁפֹּט:

2 עַד־מָתַי תִּשְׁפְּטוּ־עָוֶל
וּפְנֵי רְשָׁעִים תִּשְׂאוּ־סֶלָה:
3 שִׁפְטוּ־דַל וְיָתוֹם
עָנִי וָרָשׁ הַצְדִּיקוּ:
4 פַּלְּטוּ־דַל וְאֶבְיוֹן
מִיַּד רְשָׁעִים הַצִּילוּ:

5 לֹא יָדְעוּ | וְלֹא יָבִינוּ
בַּחֲשֵׁכָה יִתְהַלָּכוּ
יִמּוֹטוּ כָּל־מוֹסְדֵי אָרֶץ:
6 אֲנִי־אָמַרְתִּי אֱלֹהִים אַתֶּם
וּבְנֵי עֶלְיוֹן כֻּלְּכֶם:
7 אָכֵן כְּאָדָם תְּמוּתוּן
וּכְאַחַד הַשָּׂרִים תִּפֹּלוּ:

8 קוּמָה אֱלֹהִים שָׁפְטָה הָאָרֶץ
כִּי־אַתָּה תִנְחַל בְּכָל־הַגּוֹיִם:

Psalm 94:1–95:3 for Wednesday

1 God of vengeances, Adonai!
God of vengeances, shine forth!
2 Raise Yourself up, Judge of the earth,
Render recompense to the arrogant!

3 How long shall the wicked, Adonai,
How long shall the wicked exult?
4 When they speak, they spew forth disdain;
All the doers of iniquity act boastfully.
5 They crush Your people, Adonai,
They afflict Your heritage,
6 They strangle widow and stranger,
And commit murder on those without fathers;
7 They say, Yah will not see,
The God of Jacob will not pay heed.

8 *You* pay proper heed, you boorish people,
And you fools—when will you wise up?
9 Will the One who implants the ear not hear?
Will the One who shapes the eye not look?
10 Will the One who chastises the nations not
   reprove,
Especially the One who teaches human beings
   knowledge?

11 Adonai knows human thoughts—
That they are vapor.

12 Happy the person whom Yah chastises,
And teaches from Your Torah,
13 To give rest from days of suffering
Until a pit is dug for the wicked.

תהילים פרקים 94:1–95:3

1 אֵל־נְקָמוֹת יְיָ
אֵל נְקָמוֹת הוֹפִיעַ:
2 הִנָּשֵׂא שֹׁפֵט הָאָרֶץ
הָשֵׁב גְּמוּל עַל־גֵּאִים:

3 עַד־מָתַי רְשָׁעִים | יְיָ
עַד־מָתַי רְשָׁעִים יַעֲלֹזוּ:
4 יַבִּיעוּ יְדַבְּרוּ עָתָק
יִתְאַמְּרוּ כָּל־פֹּעֲלֵי אָוֶן:
5 עַמְּךָ יְיָ יְדַכְּאוּ
וְנַחֲלָתְךָ יְעַנּוּ:
6 אַלְמָנָה וְגֵר יַהֲרֹגוּ
וִיתוֹמִים יְרַצֵּחוּ:
7 וַיֹּאמְרוּ לֹא יִרְאֶה־יָּהּ
וְלֹא־יָבִין אֱלֹהֵי יַעֲקֹב:

8 בִּינוּ בֹּעֲרִים בָּעָם
וּכְסִילִים מָתַי תַּשְׂכִּילוּ:
9 הֲנֹטַע אֹזֶן הֲלֹא יִשְׁמָע
אִם־יֹצֵר עַיִן הֲלֹא יַבִּיט:
10 הֲיֹסֵר גּוֹיִם הֲלֹא יוֹכִיחַ
הַמְלַמֵּד אָדָם דָּעַת:

11 יְיָ יֹדֵעַ מַחְשְׁבוֹת אָדָם
כִּי־הֵמָּה הָבֶל:

12 אַשְׁרֵי | הַגֶּבֶר אֲשֶׁר־תְּיַסְּרֶנּוּ יָּהּ
וּמִתּוֹרָתְךָ תְלַמְּדֶנּוּ:
13 לְהַשְׁקִיט לוֹ מִימֵי רָע
עַד יִכָּרֶה לָרָשָׁע שָׁחַת:

14 For Adonai will not forsake the people,
Nor abandon their inheritance.
15 For judgments shall again be made with justice,
And all the upright in heart shall go after it.

16 Who will rise up for me among the evildoers?
Who will stand up for me among the doers of
   iniquity?
17 Unless Adonai had been a help for me
I would have been ready to lie down in silence.
18 If I were to say, "My foot is slipping!"
Your covenantal love, Adonai, would support me.
19 When disquieting thoughts rage inside me,
Your comforting brings me joy.

20 Shall the seat of destruction make alliance
   with You
As it shapes mischief through law?
21 They mount an attack against the most just
   person,
And condemn the person of innocent blood.
22 But Adonai has been a fortress for me,
And my God the rock of my refuge.
23 You will bring back their iniquity upon them,
And put an end to them in their wickedness—
Adonai our God will put an end to them.

95:1 Come, let's sing to God!
Let's make a *t'ruah* sound before the Rock of our
   deliverance!
2 Let's walk thankfully into God's presence
With singing, with *t'ruah* sounds,
Meant just for You:
3 A great God is Adonai,
The great ruler over all those
Whom we permit to rule over us.

14 כִּי | לֹא־יִטֹּשׁ יְיָ עַמּוֹ
וְנַחֲלָתוֹ לֹא יַעֲזֹב:
15 כִּי־עַד־צֶדֶק יָשׁוּב מִשְׁפָּט
וְאַחֲרָיו כָּל־יִשְׁרֵי־לֵב:

16 מִי־יָקוּם לִי עִם־מְרֵעִים
מִי־יִתְיַצֵּב לִי עִם־פֹּעֲלֵי אָוֶן:
17 לוּלֵי יְיָ עֶזְרָתָה לִּי
כִּמְעַט | שָׁכְנָה דוּמָה נַפְשִׁי:
18 אִם־אָמַרְתִּי מָטָה רַגְלִי
חַסְדְּךָ יְיָ יִסְעָדֵנִי:
19 בְּרֹב שַׂרְעַפַּי בְּקִרְבִּי
תַּנְחוּמֶיךָ יְשַׁעַשְׁעוּ נַפְשִׁי:

20 הַיְחָבְרְךָ כִּסֵּא הַוּוֹת
יֹצֵר עָמָל עֲלֵי־חֹק:
21 יָגוֹדּוּ עַל־נֶפֶשׁ צַדִּיק
וְדָם נָקִי יַרְשִׁיעוּ:
22 וַיְהִי יְיָ לִי לְמִשְׂגָּב
וֵאלֹהַי לְצוּר מַחְסִי:
23 וַיָּשֶׁב עֲלֵיהֶם | אֶת־אוֹנָם
וּבְרָעָתָם יַצְמִיתֵם
יַצְמִיתֵם יְיָ אֱלֹהֵינוּ:

95:1 לְכוּ נְרַנְּנָה לַיְיָ
נָרִיעָה לְצוּר יִשְׁעֵנוּ:
2 נְקַדְּמָה פָנָיו בְּתוֹדָה
בִּזְמִרוֹת נָרִיעַ לוֹ:
3 כִּי אֵל גָּדוֹל יְיָ
וּמֶלֶךְ גָּדוֹל עַל־כָּל־אֱלֹהִים:

Psalm 81 for Thursday

1 For the conductor upon the *gitit*, of Asaph.

2 Let joyful song ring out to God, our strength,
Ring out *t'ruah* to the God of Jacob!
3 Raise a song, celebrate on the drum,
A lyre and a lute making sweet harmonies
     together!
4 Sound *t'kiah* on the shofar at the New Month,
When the moon is still hidden on our festive day!
5 For it is a statute for Israel,
A law by the God of Jacob.
6 You appointed it as testimony for Joseph
When You went forth against the land of Egypt,
Language I did not know would I divine:

7 "I removed his shoulder from the burden,
His hands were transferred from the weighty
     basket.
8 In trouble you called, and I rescued you,
I answered you in the place where thunder hides;
I tried you at the waters of Meribah—selah!
9 Hear, My people, and I will testify to you,
Israel—if you would listen to Me!
10 There shall be no strange god with you,
Nor shall you bow down to any foreign god.
11 I am Adonai your God
Who is bringing you up from the Land of Egypt;
Open wide your mouth and I shall fill it.

12 "But My people did not listen to My voice,
Israel would have none of Me.
13 So I let them go in the stubbornness of their
     heart,
That they might walk according to their own
     counsels.

תהילים פרק 81

1 לַמְנַצֵּחַ | עַל־הַגִּתִּית לְאָסָף:

2 הַרְנִינוּ לֵאלֹהִים עוּזֵּנוּ
הָרִיעוּ לֵאלֹהֵי יַעֲקֹב:

3 שְׂאוּ־זִמְרָה וּתְנוּ־תֹף
כִּנּוֹר נָעִים עִם־נָבֶל:

4 תִּקְעוּ בַחֹדֶשׁ שׁוֹפָר
בַּכֶּסֶה לְיוֹם חַגֵּנוּ:

5 כִּי חֹק לְיִשְׂרָאֵל הוּא
מִשְׁפָּט לֵאלֹהֵי יַעֲקֹב:

6 עֵדוּת | בִּיהוֹסֵף שָׂמוֹ
בְּצֵאתוֹ עַל־אֶרֶץ מִצְרָיִם
שְׂפַת לֹא־יָדַעְתִּי אֶשְׁמָע:

7 הֲסִירוֹתִי מִסֵּבֶל שִׁכְמוֹ
כַּפָּיו מִדּוּד תַּעֲבֹרְנָה:

8 בַּצָּרָה קָרָאתָ וָאֲחַלְּצֶךָּ
אֶעֶנְךָ בְּסֵתֶר רַעַם
אֶבְחָנְךָ עַל־מֵי מְרִיבָה סֶלָה:

9 שְׁמַע עַמִּי וְאָעִידָה בָּךְ
יִשְׂרָאֵל אִם־תִּשְׁמַע־לִי:

10 לֹא־יִהְיֶה בְךָ אֵל זָר
וְלֹא תִשְׁתַּחֲוֶה לְאֵל נֵכָר:

11 אָנֹכִי | יְיָ אֱלֹהֶיךָ
הַמַּעַלְךָ מֵאֶרֶץ מִצְרָיִם
הַרְחֶב־פִּיךָ וַאֲמַלְאֵהוּ:

12 וְלֹא־שָׁמַע עַמִּי לְקוֹלִי
וְיִשְׂרָאֵל לֹא־אָבָה לִי:

13 וָאֲשַׁלְּחֵהוּ בִּשְׁרִירוּת לִבָּם
יֵלְכוּ בְּמוֹעֲצוֹתֵיהֶם:

14 "Oh that My people would listen to Me,
That Israel would walk in My ways!
15 In a little while I would extirpate their enemies,
I would turn My hand against their oppressors;
16 Those who hate Adonai shall come cringing to
   the Holy One,
And such a time will last forever for them.

17 "As for Israel, I shall feed him from the fat of
   wheat,
And with honey from the rock will I satisfy him."

14 לוּ עַמִּי שֹׁמֵעַ לִי
יִשְׂרָאֵל בִּדְרָכַי יְהַלֵּכוּ:
15 כִּמְעַט אוֹיְבֵיהֶם אַכְנִיעַ
וְעַל צָרֵיהֶם אָשִׁיב יָדִי:
16 מְשַׂנְאֵי יְיָ יְכַחֲשׁוּ־לוֹ
וִיהִי עִתָּם לְעוֹלָם:

17 וַיַּאֲכִילֵהוּ מֵחֵלֶב חִטָּה
וּמִצּוּר דְּבַשׁ אַשְׂבִּיעֶךָ:

Psalm 93 for Friday

1 Adonai is Sovereign,
Robed in nobility!
Robed is Adonai,
Girded with strength.
Now the world is set firm,
It will not be shaken;
2 As Your throne was set firm since the beginning
   of time,
You have been
Forever.

3 Though the rivers leap up, Adonai,
The rivers leap up full-voiced,
Though the rivers leap up in crashing cadence—
4 More powerful than their sound,
Than the crash of all the mighty breakers of the
   sea below,
Is the might on high of Adonai.

5 Your testimonies are very faithful.
Holy beauty will curtain Your house,
Adonai,
For long days,
Long, long days.

תהילים פרק 93

1 יְיָ מָלָךְ גֵּאוּת לָבֵשׁ
לָבֵשׁ יְיָ עֹז הִתְאַזָּר
אַף־תִּכּוֹן תֵּבֵל בַּל־תִּמּוֹט:
2 נָכוֹן כִּסְאֲךָ מֵאָז
מֵעוֹלָם אָתָּה:

3 נָשְׂאוּ נְהָרוֹת | יְיָ
נָשְׂאוּ נְהָרוֹת קוֹלָם
יִשְׂאוּ נְהָרוֹת דָּכְיָם:
4 מִקֹּלוֹת | מַיִם רַבִּים
אַדִּירִים מִשְׁבְּרֵי־יָם
אַדִּיר בַּמָּרוֹם יְיָ:

5 עֵדֹתֶיךָ | נֶאֶמְנוּ מְאֹד
לְבֵיתְךָ נַאֲוָה־קֹדֶשׁ
יְיָ לְאֹרֶךְ יָמִים:

Psalm 92 for Shabbat/Saturday

1 A psalm, a song of the Day of Shabbat.
2 It is good to offer thanks to Adonai
And to sing to Your name, Most High,
3 To tell tales of Your covenantal love in the morning
And Your faithfulness in the nights
4 On a ten-string and on a lute,
On meditative strumming of a lyre.
5 For You have given me joy through Your acts;
Of the work of Your hands I shall sing:
6 "How great are Your works, Adonai,
How very deep Your thoughts."

7 An ignorant man will not know,
A fool will not understand this:
8 When wicked people sprout up like grass
And all the doers of iniquity peep through the ground—
They will be stamped out for eternity,
9 But You are on high forever, Adonai!
10 For behold, Your foes, Adonai,
For behold, Your foes shall fall away—
All the workers of iniquity shall be scattered.

11 But You hold up my horn like a hoary ox,
I luxuriate in scented oils.
12 My eye can spot those who are watching me,
My ear detects the evildoers rising up against me.
13 A just person sprouts up like the palm,
Growing tall like a cedar in the Lebanon,
14 Planted in the House of Adonai,
They will sprout nobly in the courts of our God.
15 They shall be fruitful even in old age,
Green and luxuriant shall they be,
16 Branching out in tales of the uprightness of Adonai:
"My Rock,
In whom no imperfection can be found."

תהילים פרק 92

1 מִזְמוֹר שִׁיר לְיוֹם הַשַּׁבָּת:

2 טוֹב לְהֹדוֹת לַיְיָ
וּלְזַמֵּר לְשִׁמְךָ עֶלְיוֹן:

3 לְהַגִּיד בַּבֹּקֶר חַסְדֶּךָ
וֶאֱמוּנָתְךָ בַּלֵּילוֹת:

4 עֲלֵי־עָשׂוֹר וַעֲלֵי־נָבֶל
עֲלֵי הִגָּיוֹן בְּכִנּוֹר:

5 כִּי שִׂמַּחְתַּנִי יְיָ בְּפָעֳלֶךָ
בְּמַעֲשֵׂי יָדֶיךָ אֲרַנֵּן:

6 מַה־גָּדְלוּ מַעֲשֶׂיךָ יְיָ
מְאֹד עָמְקוּ מַחְשְׁבֹתֶיךָ:

7 אִישׁ־בַּעַר לֹא יֵדָע
וּכְסִיל לֹא־יָבִין אֶת־זֹאת:

8 בִּפְרֹחַ רְשָׁעִים | כְּמוֹ עֵשֶׂב
וַיָּצִיצוּ כָּל־פֹּעֲלֵי אָוֶן
לְהִשָּׁמְדָם עֲדֵי־עַד:

9 וְאַתָּה מָרוֹם לְעֹלָם יְיָ:

10 כִּי הִנֵּה אֹיְבֶיךָ | יְיָ
כִּי־הִנֵּה אֹיְבֶיךָ יֹאבֵדוּ
יִתְפָּרְדוּ כָּל־פֹּעֲלֵי אָוֶן:

11 וַתָּרֶם כִּרְאֵים קַרְנִי בַּלֹּתִי בְּשֶׁמֶן רַעֲנָן:

12 וַתַּבֵּט עֵינִי בְּשׁוּרָי
בַּקָּמִים עָלַי מְרֵעִים תִּשְׁמַעְנָה אָזְנָי:

13 צַדִּיק כַּתָּמָר יִפְרָח כְּאֶרֶז בַּלְּבָנוֹן יִשְׂגֶּה:

14 שְׁתוּלִים בְּבֵית יְיָ בְּחַצְרוֹת אֱלֹהֵינוּ יַפְרִיחוּ:

15 עוֹד יְנוּבוּן בְּשֵׂיבָה דְּשֵׁנִים וְרַעֲנַנִּים יִהְיוּ:

16 לְהַגִּיד כִּי־יָשָׁר יְיָ צוּרִי וְלֹא־עַוְלָתָה בּוֹ:

Reflections for Focus
Shir Shel Yom Psalms

Week 1

Rabbi Yosei bar Y'hudah,
of K'far HaBavli in the Galilee,
an area well suited to vineyards,
suggests
sacred texts are similar to wine aging in a cask.

Unlike ripe grapes eaten from the vine,
with time wine takes on nuance,
as new faces, facets, and flavors
emerge and blend together.

Aged, it tastes
new each day
when we drink it, sip by sip.

Sunday, Week 1   *Psalm 24:1*

Lamed Leads the Way

לְדָוִד מִזְמוֹר לַיְיָ הָאָרֶץ וּמְלוֹאָהּ תֵּבֵל וְיֹשְׁבֵי בָהּ:

Of David: A song.
To God belongs the earth and its fullness,
The world, and those who dwell within it.

The psalm begins with the letter *lamed*.
L'David, of David,
indicating supposed authorship of this song,
or at least attribution, to King David.

Lamed leads from this spot in many psalms.
These first words are like opening credits or instructions.
They grow familiar like
clutter on a desk,
magnets on the refrigerator.
We push along, rush along,
ready to enter, to engage with the psalm itself,
to see its secrets and our challenges,
its surprises and our obstacles.

The song may be of David,
but the earth, the world, the rivers, the seasons,
the mountains and the holy places
(and what place made by God is not holy?),
they are all of God.
L'Adonai.

ל–*Lamed.*
The tallest among the 22 Hebrew letters,
positioned in the alphabet like a fulcrum.
Its shape-shifting neighbors,
כ, *kaf* with its flat bottom, and
מ, *mem*'s sturdy triangle,
both stay within the lines.
Lamed balances on a single tiny tip.
Through deep unseen roots it drinks
from primordial seas, rivers flowing still from Eden.
It stretches majestically,
up, up, and up toward the sky,
into the universe,
out to God.

L'Adonai.
It's almost a one-word psalm.
It's [all] of God.

We can learn from the *lamed.*
We can ascend to holy places,
with clean hands and honest hearts,
standing tall as caretakers,
rising to protect our planet,
ensuring the delicate balance that is needed
to keep icebergs frozen and seas from rising,
rains from flooding fields,
and the sun from scorching sustenance.
It's our imperative,
our entryway to the gates of God's Presence,
the gates of Eternity.

with each psalm on its day.

Monday, Week 1 *Psalm 48:6*

Blue Gloves

הֵמָּה רָאוּ כֵּן תָּמֵהוּ נִבְהֲלוּ נֶחְפָּזוּ׃

They saw, indeed they were amazed—
They rushed to and fro in terror!

Jewish Publication Society translation:
At the mere sight of it they were stunned,
they were terrified, they panicked.

For Kate Corliss, Old King's Coffeehouse, West Yarmouth, Massachusetts, March 22, 2020.

This time the angel wears blue gloves.
Her hands reach into the walk-in cooler, pulling out
signature English muffins, tubs of sliced meat and cheese,
famous homemade black bean salsa.
She is not serving lunch.

With well-practiced choreography, she sets
gallons of milk, quarts of cream,
dozens of eggs, loaves of bread on the counter.
She is not serving breakfast.

My mind darts this way and that,
unsettled and terrified.
I am
worried about this one,
protective of that one,
needing to reach another.
Resources, financial, medical—
hopefully not spiritual—
could be depleted.
People will die.
Lots of people.
More people than we can count.
Panic nearly paralyzes me.
The angel surely feels it too:

. . . to remember, to thank, to praise

a new business—shuttered,
pounds of coffee waiting to be ground,
the spring schedule for doughnuts ready.
In her kitchen there is no running or rushing,
at the altar of the counter, no alarm or terror.
Her warm smile matches the boots on her feet.
She wears them for walking, dreaming, thriving,
surviving.

She spreads what she has, like sweet frosting.
No milk poured down the drain,
no meat tossed in the trash,
no bread crumbled for birds.
No hoarding, only sharing
fresh food, to be served by more angels,
with a side of love.

A stillness fills the space.
The espresso hisses in the press,
the steamer exhales,
and so do I,
as she froths milk.

God's messenger serves
holy hospitality and godlike generosity.
I inhale compassion, sweet as sugar.
The first small sip warms my frozen, fearful soul.
We raise cups to toast,
even with lids on they seem to overflow.
We sip slowly,
to sustain us for we don't know how long.
I am calm and steady,
like the angel in the blue gloves,
calmly filling cups with compassion,
for a moment.

> In Hebrew, the word for both angel and messenger is *malach* (מַלְאָךְ).

with each psalm on its day.

Tuesday, Week 1   *Psalm 82:1*

Proper Posture

מִזְמוֹר לְאָסָף אֱלֹהִים נִצָּב בַּעֲדַת־אֵל בְּקֶרֶב אֱלֹהִים יִשְׁפֹּט:
A psalm of Asaph.
God stands up in a godly congregation,
Passing judgment in the midst of godlike judges.

Tuesday begins with proper posture.
Elohim nitzav.
Stand like God.
Perhaps Mountain Pose, feet rooted in the ground?
Or maybe Warrior Pose, arms extended?
Hands pressed in prayer is not enough.
Certainly no clenched fists or crossed arms.
Stand or perhaps sit, long spine, connecting earth and sky.

The breath flows long and slow, and then fast and short,
as closed eyes open to see.
The list of people reads like the plagues in the *Haggadah:*
   דַּל *Dal*—lowly
   יָתוֹם *Yatom*—orphans
   עָנִי *Oni*—afflicted
   רָשׁ *Rash*—poor
   more *Dal*—more bent souls
   אֶבְיוֹן *Evyon*—needy

The ancient words are real,
the people and the litany overwhelm.
I see each one—
each category, each person, each act of cruel injustice.
And I know each act of rescue, of redemption, of help,
must be unique
to stay the hands of the wicked,
to turn these worlds toward justice.
But on Tuesday my week is already full,

where will I find, how will I find,
the time, the strength, the courage, the hope,
the partners to do this work.

B'nei Elyon kulchem.
B'not Elyon kulchen.
I, one of many children of God, take up the pose.
It's the pose of leaders,
ready (or not) for the challenge in the deepest darkness.
I can do this; we can do this:
Teach.
Lo yadu v'lo yavinu,
Teach—
one who doesn't yet know,
one who does not yet understand,
in our tottering world,
there is a vision of a better one, a Just One,
and the transformation begins.

In a whisper, with a shout,
with audacity and urgency, I return with the Psalmist to the posture.
Kumah Elohim!
Rise.
An essential call to God,
to ourselves, and to each other.
Get up, images and agents of the Most High!
Get to work on a Tuesday and keep working!
Time on earth is limited
and the needs are unending,
but the human capacity
for seeking justice
is vast.
The earth and all in the world depend on You,
and me, to stand.

with each psalm on its day.

Wednesday, Week 1   *Psalm 94:1*

God of Vengeance

אֵל־נְקָמוֹת יְיָ אֵל נְקָמוֹת הוֹפִיעַ:

God of vengeances, Adonai!
God of vengeances, shine forth!

I don't like this name for God,
God of Vengeance.
I resist reading the psalm with its
repetitive,
emphatic,
opening.

Where is the Holy One I prefer:
God of All Creation
My Rock
Healer of Broken Hearts
Giver of Torah
even, Judge of Truth?

Then, I read.
I realize,
we are multifaceted like our God.
We humans are
creators,
rock-solid friends,
healers of the sick,
teachers of Torah,
judges in court and on the street.
We are also seekers of revenge,
like our God.

The instinct is all too familiar.
When feelings are bruised,
cruel words are spoken,
a heart or a trust are broken,

violence overtakes the voice,
we want to take revenge.

We say,
He hurt me . . .
She hurt someone I love . . .
They hurt our relationship . . .
I'll show them.
I'll do the same, or worse, in return.
We rationalize, we justify,
it's in the name of God.

Suddenly it's obvious.
We have the capacity, like God,
for vengeance and revenge.
And we have our other God-given gifts:
knowledge, compassion, integrity, patience.
Amidst evil, iniquity, and inequity
we can choose, in moments of rage,
of desperation and deep darkness,
not an eye for an eye or a tooth for a tooth,
but to judge with justice,
to rise with restraint,
to help with an upright heart.

We can return the courts to places
where their evidence is not suppressed,
where the color of his skin does not prejudice a jury,
where beauty does not make her at fault.
Made in the image of the God of Vengeance
we are empowered to reestablish courts where
"the judgments made by human judges
shall once more approach the ideal rightness of justice."
It is time,
to choose what is holy
and set right what is wrong,
so justice will reign, again.

with each psalm on its day.

Thursday, Week 1   *Psalm 81:7*

Weight Off My Shoulders

הֲסִירוֹתִי מִסֵּבֶל שִׁכְמוֹ כַּפָּיו מִדּוּד תַּעֲבֹרְנָה:

"I removed his shoulder from the burden,
His hands were transferred from the weighty basket."

"It's such a weight off my shoulders."
We say it all the time—when we have
finished a big project,
met a massive responsibility,
made a difficult choice,
let nature take its course.

We say it because of the *seivel*,
the oppression, the burden, the weight,
the load—physical, emotional, spiritual—of life.
We feel our shoulder muscles,
the ones that knit themselves to our necks,
causing our chins to drop and our heads to hang, tighten.
Our shoulder blades compress
rather than spread wide, like angel wings.
Our shoulders hunch up and our backs bend,
under the burden of the *seivel*.
But then, sometimes, we finish something,
the *seivel* is
shed like a snake's skin,
left behind like flotsam on the seashore,
and we move on.

We focus on the weight we carry on our shoulders.
But not the Psalmist,
and not God.
The Psalmist writes that God says,
"I removed his shoulder from the burden"

not,
I removed the burden from the shoulder.
The focus is different—
the person is changed
and the weight remains.

Seivel—
labor, decisions, dilemmas,
challenges of leadership, of learning,
of life—
endures.
We will return to our loads, again and again,
tomorrow or next Thursday, or after Shabbat,
but our shoulders can't bear the constant weight,
cauldrons, baskets, buckets—
physical or metaphorical.

The burdens of the world are constants,
but our shoulders must rest.
A reminder on a Thursday that Shabbat is coming.
A reminder built into the structure of the universe,
our world and our lives,
we need a time of rest.
With our ego's need to be loved and fed constantly,
we resist.
But God insists.
And so do we,
even if not of our own accord.
The weight will be lifted,
I will return
strong, refreshed, ready to take up the load—
to hear God's voice,
to raise my voice in song.

Friday, Week 1   Psalm 93:1

Dress Like God

יְהֹוָה מָלָךְ גֵּאוּת לָבֵשׁ לָבֵשׁ יְיָ עֹז הִתְאַזָּר
אַף־תִּכּוֹן תֵּבֵל בַּל־תִּמּוֹט:

Adonai is Sovereign,
Robed in nobility!
Robed is Adonai,
Girded with strength.
Now the world is set firm,
It will not be shaken.

I never imagined the Rabbis of the Talmud as fashionistas,
until I encountered Rabbi Chanina.
He holds his own with the fashion correspondents
at the red carpet of the twenty-first-century Oscars.
He watches with awe,
as many images of One God appear.
He blesses the beauty of the body,
celebrates the infinite innovations,
looks for what will endure.
He raises his gaze to notice,
there are some with beautiful bodies
wearing clothes that are not flattering,
and others with beautiful clothes
not at all suited to their bodies.

His fashion commentary concludes:
God is always beautiful
and divine clothing is always perfect,
in every moment.
God wears:
Majesty for the parting of the Red Sea.
Strength when giving Torah at Sinai.

Vengeance to do battle with enemies.
Righteousness to serve as Judge.
Zeal to keep Jewish life vibrant.
A crimson cloak to evoke the possibility of change.
Raiments of white to proclaim the arrival of peace.

Every day God dresses in nobility
accessorized with stability
to balance an ever-shifting world.
As I get dressed every day, I ask myself,
What should I wear today?
Does God ask this question at dawn
as the Holy One dresses in glory and majesty
and wraps light as a garment?

I want to follow Rabbi Chanina's fashion advice
and see myself as radiant
in my imperfect body
no matter what I wear.
On the red carpet of my life,
I can be like God, steady and firm footed,
robed in the right garment for each sacred action.
I will dress each day
as if wrapped in light,
and raise my voice,
in chorus with the rivers and the seas
with gratitude to God,
for a world garbed in holy beauty.

with each psalm on its day.

Shabbat/Saturday, Week 1   *Psalm 92:3, 16*

Tell a Story

לְהַגִּיד בַּבֹּקֶר חַסְדֶּךָ וֶאֱמוּנָתְךָ בַּלֵּילוֹת:
לְהַגִּיד כִּי־יָשָׁר יְיָ צוּרִי וְלֹא־עַוְלָתָה בּוֹ:

To tell tales of Your covenantal love [chesed] *in the
morning
And Your faithfulness* [emunah] *in the nights. . . .*

Branching out in tales of the uprightness [yashar] *of
Adonai:
"My Rock,
In whom no imperfection can be found."*

Shabbat is story time.
A full day to speak
of beliefs, spirit-full relationships,
mystical and magical moments,
fleeting like daybreak
or long-lasting like the night.

Tell a story, at dawn.
When the world and the week are new and fresh,
it's a story of *chesed*,
a morning whisper of covenantal love,
God's abiding kindness.
A song of gratitude rises like the sun,
God's generous love,
always available.

Tell a story as the sun sets.
As the week concludes, choose a tale of *emunah*,
an evening affirmation of God's faithfulness.
Testimony to God's belief in,
and loyalty to,
us.

. . . to remember, to thank, to praise

No matter how lonely life feels,
God does not abandon us.

Tell a story,
to yourself,
to anyone who will listen,
to the trees,
or a Rock.

Branch out your tale of the uprightness of *Adonai*.
Fairy tale or autobiography,
old or aspirational.
Tell a story about a God,
reaching up and around you
like branches of the tree.
Or maybe a story about yourself,
made in the image of God,
with eyes that see, ears that hear;
with deep roots,
standing tall,
bearing fruit,
yashar, upright in the face of challenge.

Tell a story that begins,
"Once upon a time . . ."
Or perhaps,
"With God as my Rock . . ."
Maybe it ends,
"happily ever after"
or instead,
"in whom no imperfection is found."
Try a one-word story.
Tzuri—God is my Rock:
sheltering me with *chesed*,
embracing me with *emunah*,
allowing me to stand, *yashar*, upright.

with each psalm on its day.

Week 2

Rabbi Chiya bar Abba,
in the name of his teacher Rabbi Yochanan,
teaches:
Sacred texts grow like figs.

Wherever we search the tree for figs to eat
we find newly ripened fruit.
The figs don't all ripen at once.

There is always something
new each day
to find.

Sunday, Week 2   *Psalm 24:3–5*

Clean Hands Carry Blessings

מִי־יַעֲלֶה בְהַר־יְיָ וּמִי־יָקוּם בִּמְקוֹם קָדְשׁוֹ:
נְקִי כַפַּיִם וּבַר־לֵבָב אֲשֶׁר
לֹא־נָשָׂא לַשָּׁוְא נַפְשִׁי וְלֹא נִשְׁבַּע לְמִרְמָה:
יִשָּׂא בְרָכָה מֵאֵת יְיָ וּצְדָקָה מֵאֱלֹהֵי יִשְׁעוֹ:

*Who shall ascend to the mountain of Adonai
And who shall stand at Your sacred site?
[One with] clean hands shall, and [one of] an honest heart;
One who raises up no falsehood to deface My name;
Who has not sworn an oath that hides deceit—
This one shall raise up a blessing from Adonai
And justice from the God of our deliverance.*

A Sunday psalm, an any-day psalm, an everyday psalm,
an all-day psalm during a pandemic.
Instruction, encouragement, inspiration,
from an ancient world to a modern time.
The earth and all its continents, the seas and all their shores,
all of us everywhere,
and each disease,
God made them all.

All share this miraculous universe,
where we are blessed and challenged:
To live and learn, care and cure,
do no harm.
To love and lose, cry and comfort,
heal the harm.
To do what's right and just and fair, and prudent,
with strength and patience and dignity.

Partners with our Creator
we battle against a relentless foe,
unseen but deeply felt, both microscopic and global.
A feared enemy at the gates,
in our homes and schools and stores,
synagogues, mosques, and churches—
like God it knows no borders, sees no differences.
We fight together with heads raised—not hunkered down.
Feet grounded by gravity, rooted in the enduring facts of nature,
clean hands lead to blessings.

We wash our hands and inspect our hearts—
an opportunity, over and again, to breathe,
and recite these words, taped above the sink:

Who will stand in a holy place?
I will.
With clean hands.
With an open heart.
I can bring blessing from God,
deliver justice for all people.
Like God I am strong.
With God I can open gates of healing and hope.

בָּרוּךְ אַתָּה, יְיָ אֱלֹהֵינוּ, רוּחַ הָעוֹלָם,
אֲשֶׁר קִדְּשָׁנוּ בְּמִצְוֹתָיו וְצִוָּנוּ עַל נְטִילַת יָדָיִם.
Baruch atah, Adonai Eloheinu, Ruach haolam,
asher kid'shanu b'mitzvotav vitzivanu al n'tilat yadayim.

Blessed are You *Adonai*, Breath of the universe,
for giving us the sacred opportunity to lift up our hands
toward blessing.

This heart, these hands, my Breath opens healing gates for Holiness to
enter.

with each psalm on its day.

Monday, Week 2   *Psalm 48:8*

God's East Wind

בְּרוּחַ קָדֵים תְּשַׁבֵּר אֳנִיּוֹת תַּרְשֵׁישׁ:
With but a wind sent from the east
You smash the ships of Tarshish.

Where I live, the wind mostly blows from the west.
Clouds cluster, the day darkens, and the rain pounds.
The storm charges through and makes its way east.
Once, the sky glowed green, humming filled the air.
The west winds twisted themselves together,
touching the ground,
traveling straight from west to east,
hungry.
Feeding first on a school cafeteria and classrooms,
gobbling an entire grocery story,
swallowing hundreds of kitchens (and their homes),
consuming plants in a nursery for its dessert
along a single swath.

Some live where storms blow from the south,
smashing their way up the coast.
Others know the north wind,
icy blasts that blow with blankets of snow.
Too many people know a shifting wind,
fueling fires in fields and forests.
But the east wind is different.
It blows across lands and seas,
in many lifetimes and any season.

God's East Wind breaks the strongest ships
with skilled sailors at the helm, laden with luxuries.
A divine message in Ezekiel's voice: Beware of arrogance and greed.

. . . to remember, to thank, to praise

God's East Wind is a breeze, gentle and steady in the sun,
air so parched, a prophet wishes for death.
God goads Jonah: Embrace your capacity to change.

God's East Wind blows day and night,
locusts at dawn, a plague.
A message to a Pharaoh: Soften your hard heart.

God's East Wind has gale force,
pushing water into walls all night.
A miraculous path for Moses and Miriam:
Fear, faith, and freedom await.

God's East Wind blows around the world.
Beware of greed and arrogance.
Be open to the potential to change.
Have a soft and open heart.
Be ready to cross the sea.
All the wind's blessings are God,
Ruach Elohim, Breath, Wind of the universe,
present at Creation, blowing for the Psalmist,
in our lives,
forever.

with each psalm on its day.

Tuesday, Week 2   *Psalm 82:2*

The Judge

עַד־מָתַי תִּשְׁפְּטוּ־עָוֶל וּפְנֵי רְשָׁעִים תִּשְׂאוּ־סֶלָה:
"How long will you judge unjustly,
Raising up the face of the wicked—selah!"

I judged myself, a long time ago and for a long time,
harshly, unfairly.
I judged myself, dismissed the evidence,
issued the verdict:
lacking.
Not smart enough,
not funny enough,
not the right gender or size or of the right lineage.
I was incarcerated
by my own imagination, biases, insecurity.

In another court, on another day,
someone else judged me more fairly.
A godlike judge saw me and overturned my opinion.
I was judged:
worthy.
Smart enough,
strong enough,
kind enough.
One could not be found guilty:
of being a woman, or small, or for having only one parent.

Not a lawyer, I am my own advocate, and always in court.
Most of yesterday.
Only once so far today.
Likely again tomorrow.
On the bench passing judgment on myself:
in the court of the mind,

in front of the mirror,
at the kitchen table,
in the office or classroom,
in public and in private.
It's the same case, tried over and over.
But not anymore.
It is time to judge more justly,
not only others, but myself.
It is time to raise my face of accomplishment and kindness,
of creativity and strength.
It's obvious to me fairness is due to all,
and now to myself as well.
All of us are worthy of fair judgment in a court of law.
I am worthy of fair judgment, in the depths of my souls,
in the presence of the Judge Who Stands,
Steady in the Darkness, in a tottering world.

> *Leviticus 19:15*
> You shall not render an unfair decision:
> do not favor the poor or show deference to the rich;
> judge your kin fairly.

with each psalm on its day.

Wednesday, Week 2   *Psalm 94:9*

Use Your Gifts

הֲבֹטַע אֹזֶן הֲלֹא יִשְׁמָע אִם־יֹצֵר עַיִן הֲלֹא יַבִּיט:

Will the One who implants the ear not hear?
Will the One who shapes the eye not look?

The gifts were given at the very beginning.
People,
shaped from clay,
animated with the breath of life,
each and all in the image of God,
endowed with miraculous gifts.

A pair of eyes refract and reflect
allowing us the ability to see—up close and far away,
to cry, to smile.
Even without them we see,
in the light and the dark,
with the imagination.
What a gift.
Eve has this gift in the Garden of Eden.
She sees the tree—that it is good for eating,
a source of sustenance for body and mind,
She eats and learns the power of making her own choices.
She shares and discovers the gift of insight.

Not one, but two delicate openings,
tiny bones and minuscule drums
enable us to hear
sounds high and low with our ears.
Even without them, or when they don't work,
we hear vibrations,
subtle and strong, noise and silence,
with the body.

What a gift.
Eve and Adam shared this gift in the Garden of Eden.
They hear the presence of their Creator,
rustling in the Garden.
They hide.
And then they learn honesty, responsibility,
hear the first sounds of life and death.

The God
who formed them and us
has no eyes and no ears but sees and hears.
We have eyes, but do we really see?
We have ears, but do we really hear?
Adam and Eve used these precious gifts in the Garden of Eden.
Can we at last—can I at least—better refine the use of these gifts?
Open ears.
Open eyes.
Open heart.
Open hands.
And with these eternal qualities I need
strength, courage, endurance, patience,
reminders—
to use them,
over and over again.

Thursday, Week 2   *Psalm 81:8*

Where Thunder Hides

בַּצָּרָה קָרָאתָ וָאֲחַלְּצֶךָ אֶעֶנְךָ בְּסֵתֶר רַעַם
אֶבְחָנְךָ עַל־מֵי מְרִיבָה סֶלָה:

In trouble you called, and I rescued you,
I answered you in the place where thunder hides;
I tried you at the waters of Meribah—selah!

The Psalmist says,
"God says . . .
'I [God] answer you [human in narrow constrained places]
from the place where thunder hides.'"

When thunder hides, is it noisy?
Compacted condensation gathering energy
to explode, to crash, to boom and echo from the sky.
Isn't it noisy, impossible to hide?

Maybe thunder is quiet when it hides.
Invisible energy silently swirling, spinning, patiently waiting.
Maybe like a bear hibernating,
to conserve power, reserve fuel.
It takes refuge
to prepare for its unique work in the world,
to roll across the sky,
echo against mountains,
hover over heads,
all part of a delicately balanced network of Life.

I've seen this silent hidden thunder.
We've all heard it,
when we stood together at Mount Sinai long ago.
The thunder emerges,
in a moment that happens in one time and place
and over and over and over, again, everywhere.

. . . to remember, to thank, to praise

When the thunder hides its sound,
in a deep silence, Revelation.

Sometimes we hear it,
sometimes we see it,
most of the time we are searching for it.
The prophet Isaiah understood.
God is not in the earthquakes or the fires,
or the thunder,
but in the hidden, silent, narrow places.
The sound within,
revealing from our hearts what is good,
what is right, what is just,
what is kind.

God speaks from where the thunder hides,
unseen and unheard,
an ever-present Presence,
breathing, waiting
to be revealed and to reveal.
And when we find it, see it, or when we hear it,
we offer blessing:

בָּרוּךְ אַתָּה, יְיָ אֱלֹהֵינוּ, מֶלֶךְ הָעוֹלָם,
שֶׁכֹּחוֹ וּגְבוּרָתוֹ מָלֵא עוֹלָם.

Baruch atah, Adonai Eloheinu, Melech haolam,
shekocho ugvurato malei olam.
Praise to You, *Adonai* our God, Sovereign of the universe,
whose power and might pervade the world.

with each psalm on its day.

Friday, Week 2   *Psalm 93:2*

Forever

נָכוֹן כִּסְאֲךָ מֵאָז מֵעוֹלָם אָתָּה:
As Your throne was set firm since the beginning
    of time,
You have been
Forever.

"From eternity You have existed"
 is one way to translate the words.
 Another is
"You have been
 Forever."

Two common Hebrew words combine,
olam and *atah*,
into a song of comfort and confidence,
as seas rage and a churning turning world
is wrapped in light and strength and steadiness.

עוֹלָם *Olam*. A noun,
meaning world or universe.
As in:
Adon Olam, a classic hymn of praise to the Creator of the universe.
Tikkun olam, an ancient call to repair the world.

עוֹלָם *Olam*. A Hebrew contranym,
a word with contradictory meanings.
Forever for the future:
God's promise to Noah, when the raging waters recede
and a rainbow rises,
never ever again, for any generation to come.
Forever, in the past:
God split a sea,
slaves stepped toward freedom and faith, long ago,

as Isaiah reflects and remembers God's name, For All Time.
The Universe, Creator of the World,
they were, they are, they will always be, One.

אַתָּה *Atah*. A pronoun.
Second person, masculine, singular.
Mundane.
You, go to the store, synagogue, school.
אַתָּה *Atah*. An intimate way to speak to the Holy.
Baruch atah, Adonai, Blessed are You, *Adonai* . . .
You, Creator, Redeemer, Giver of Torah.

We are mortal
but You, *El Olam*, God—You are eternal.
And You have been, there,
for the Psalmist who knew and affirmed You
for all who preceded the poet,
for me, for those who are yet to be.

You are Forever. Lasting. Enduring.
Always (in the past).
Forever (in the future).
Everywhere (now).
Fortitude is Your essence, God,
and perhaps, ours too.
We need it now, more than ever, to endure,
to know fourteen days, three weeks, a month, a summer,
half a year, even a whole year,
is a tiny fraction of Forever.

You made this world,
set it firm since the Beginning,
and we, if we can even be a little bit like You,
this week, this day, this hour, this minute,
then we too will endure, to see the beauty of Your house,
our house, for long days,
long long days.

Written May 1, 2020.

with each psalm on its day.

Shabbat/Saturday, Week 2   *Psalm 92:6*

It's Your Business to Make Birds

מַה־גָּדְלוּ מַעֲשֶׂיךָ יְיָ מְאֹד עָמְקוּ מַחְשְׁבֹתֶיךָ:
How great are Your works, Adonai,
How very deep Your thoughts.

How did You think,
if You even think,
of so many creations?
How did You figure out gravity?
Not Einstein's theory, but the gravity itself;
this most amazing invisible force holding us to the earth
spinning the solar system, our galaxy, and everything out there,
Beyond.
How was (or is?) it possible to imagine
infinite patterns on the leopard,
countless shapes of leaves,
so many shades of green,
and all the blues to fill the sky?

I am filled with awe,
pink clouds at dawn,
purple horizon at dusk,
red of the cardinal's wing
as the gray branches of the oak wait for buds and leaves.
A flock of the bluest birds alight on the fence,
then rise as one into the air
resting across the field
before they vanish.
Goldfinches travel thousands of miles,
arriving together to illuminate the wood outside my window.

And don't even get me started on the monarchs.
I've stood in the grove, eyes wide and ears sharp,
breathing with them,

thousands of them.
Wings pulsing, open and shut,
Once in a lifetime a sacred journey,
with an itinerary passed, from generation to generation.
All this wonder
and I've yet to contemplate
soaring mountains, crashing seas,
steaming jungles, scorching deserts, melting icebergs.

You thought of all this, shaped and animated each one,
and then,
You made us
like You.
You shared Your capacity
to think deeply,
question,
feel polar points of pain and joy,
make things.

It is Your business to make birds, not mine.
But it is my business
to think deeply and make choices that will—
as You told Adam and Eve when they received their sacred assignment—
Protect this world.
Each bird, with a near silent hum, or chirp, or incessant caw,
is a reminder
of all the wonders of the world YOU thought about,
deeply,
and then, made.
Our Inspiration,
to think,
to choose,
to praise You.

"God, how did it ever come to you to
invent Time?" (Mary Oliver)

with each psalm on its day.

Week 3

Rabbi Shmuel bar Nachmani,
among the most colorful of the Talmudic Sages,
compares
sacred texts to a mother's breast.

Whenever an infant seeks out the breast to nurse,
the baby finds milk.

The flavor is fresh,
new each day,
an ever-flowing source of nourishment.

Sunday, Week 3   *Psalm 24:5*

Raise a Flag of Blessing

יִשָּׂא בְרָכָה מֵאֵת יְיָ וּצְדָקָה מֵאֱלֹהֵי יִשְׁעוֹ:

This one shall raise up a blessing from Adonai
And justice from the God of our deliverance.

What does it mean to raise up a blessing?

Moses lifts up the heads
to count the people,
accounting for each soul.
Eyes raised up from the mud and muck at their feet,
each one a blessing of God.

Aaron and his children lift their hands,
fingers spread to shape a *shin*,
to bless the people.
"May the Divine's countenance/face/light,
presence
be raised up and shine upon you."
May you "live long and prosper."

Ancient priests lifted up sacrifices, transformed to smoke.
Today we offer up prayers.
With words of the heart, works of the hands,
in speech and song, voices raised up,
blessing rises.

The Psalmist raises up a blessing like a flag.
A banner flying aloft,
a proclamation, celebration, affirmation, identification,
for all to see,
against the sapphire blue sky,
unfurled on a divine breeze.
A blessing lifted with clean hands and a pure heart,
for justice and honor and honesty.

Symbols of blessing, each raised in declaration:
The Gates of Holiness are open!
Each gate festooned with a flag.
One for every letter of the alphabet and then some:
Amazement, beauty, and creativity.
Love, meaning, nourishment, open-heartedness,
peace.
Wisdom and wonder . . .
The gates open,
the colors fly,
and we,
in the Presence of Glorious Holiness,
raise up our blessings.

Monday, Week 3   *Psalm 48:10*

My Translation

דִּמִּ֣ינוּ אֱלֹהִ֣ים חַסְדֶּ֑ךָ בְּקֶ֝֗רֶב הֵיכָלֶֽךָ׃

We have meditated on Your covenantal love
In the innermost parts of Your Temple.

It's the kind of verse my students love.
Hebrew letters, decoded and
pronounced perfectly,
still present a puzzle.
A challenge to the reader,
each of us a translator,
to interpret,
to use the texts of our lives
to find relevance, resonance
in the text of the psalm.
Five Hebrew words,
a multitude of meanings.

We have meditated on Your covenantal love,
in the innermost parts of Your Temple.

We witnessed, O God, Your kindness,
in the midst of Your Temple.

We are awed speechless, Source of Life, by Your kindness,
as we stand in Your Temple.

We imagined Your mercy,
O God, in the midst of Your palace.

O God, we beseech Your loyalty
that we may experience Your vindication in Your Temple.

In Your Temple, God,
we meditate upon Your faithful care.

... to remember, to thank, to praise

Imagine: This verse, or any verse, comes with a label:
No Graduate Degrees Required.
Do-It-Yourself Instructions Included.
No Experience Necessary.

Try: Put them on the tongue and in the ear.
Ask: How do they feel? Are they my style? Do they reflect my values?
Will they endure, like their Inspiration?
Realize: None are the perfect fit for my heart and my head.
Wonder: Can I create my own?
Begin: Move and match combinations.
Choose a voice: Passive voice or present tense?
Select the setting: The Temple, a synagogue, the body, God's world?
Debate: What does *chesed* look like?
God's endless and gracious, compassionate forgiveness of us?
The generous kindness of Naomi to Ruth?
Reflect: Today, will I meditate or beseech or witness or imagine?

Translate:
[Fueled by Your breath]
I imagine Your loving-kindness, God,
[Flowing] in[to] the innermost place
[the heart] of Your Temple, [my body].

Tuesday, Week 3   *Psalm 82:5*

Foundations Are Tottering

לֹא יָדְעוּ ׀ וְלֹא יָבִינוּ בַּחֲשֵׁכָה יִתְהַלָּכוּ יִמּוֹטוּ כָּל־מוֹסְדֵי אָרֶץ׃

"They do not know, they do not understand
In deep darkness they stumble to and fro—
All the foundations of the earth are tottering!"

It happened one day, but it could happen any day.
Cities issued shelter-in-place laws.
Schools locked their doors on a day's notice.
The food pantry closed,
the threat of disease outweighed the threat of hunger.
Airlines wanted bailouts and small businesses too.
The bartender's hands shook as the restaurant prepared to close
    for table service.
When would she next shake a cocktail, wipe the highballs,
    gather her tips?
The waitress was unsteady on her feet.
How would her dad, a clammer who can't export black clams,
pay for oil to heat the house or gas to fuel his boat?

The world wobbles and I wonder,
Is it like:
The tremble of an earthquake, followed by devastation?
The pummeling of the shore by a winter storm, when the
    coastline collapses?
The ground shaking as a massive truck approaches, then passes
    by a moment later?

Today it is the unsteady balance of standing on a trampoline.
The fabric isn't firm.
I broaden my stance; it helps a little.
I bend my knees to lower my center of gravity; it helps a bit too.
I extend my arms for balance; this helps more.

I reach for love and compassion,
generosity, patience, and selflessness,
the enduring stabilizers of our world.
No human hands touch mine, but I'm steady,
for a moment,
in an unstable place.
Y'hudah HaLevi was right.

God is there, waiting.
On a mountaintop,
at the bottom of the sea,
under the shade of a tree,
sheltered in my home under quarantine.
When I reach out,
I find God reaching out to
steady me,
still my pounding heart,
calm my breath,
assure me,
even on the trampoline,
when the foundations of the earth are tottering,
we still stand on holy ground,
hand in hand.

Written Tuesday, March 17, 2020, in Wellfleet, Massachusetts.

with each psalm on its day.

Wednesday, Week 3   *Psalm 94:19*

Soothe the Soul

בְּרֹב שַׂרְעַפַּי בְּקִרְבִּי תַּנְחוּמֶיךָ יְשַׁעַשְׁעוּ נַפְשִׁי:
When disquieting thoughts rage inside me,
Your comforting brings me joy.

I need, we need, our world needs this psalm,
this verse, on this Wednesday morning, on any day.
"When I am tangled within, unsettled,
You comfort me, You soothe my soul."

שַׂרְעַפַּי *SaRAPai.*
A unique word in the Bible, a favorite of the troubled Job.
Perhaps a portmanteau
of two words next to each other in the dictionary.
SaRAPai is like *SaRaPH*,
from the letters *sin*, *reish*, and *pei*—to burn.
My angst, my concerns burn within me,
threaten to consume me like a fire.
SaRAPai is like *S'RaA*,
from the letters *sin*, *reish*, and *ayin*—to extend or stretch.
My worries expand,
spreading like flames fueled by dry timber,
filling my head, my heart, with fear and dread,
in the dark of the night and as the day dawns.
I am tangled in the sheets and in my mind.
I wake. I rise. I am unbalanced like the world, yesterday.

תַּנְחוּמֶיךָ *TaNCHuMechah.*
Buried within prefix and suffix, *nun*, *chet*, and *mem*,
N'CHuM—comfort.
You, God, You comfort me.
Like a:
Parent can soothe a child after a nightmare,

. . . to remember, to thank, to praise

Teacher can nourish a mind,
Friend can calm another friend,
Leader can steady a country or community,
Shepherd can shelter the flock,
Rock can give shade on a stifling day,
Breath can slow a pounding heart.

And finally, a Hebrew tongue twister,
worth practice, memorization, repetition.
Hold it in the mouth, release it from the lips,
know it, in the heart, by heart.
Two words:
three *shins*,
two silent *ayins*,
a *yod* at the beginning and at the end.
It's onomatopoeia: Shshshsh . . .

יְשַׁעַשְׁעוּ בַּפְשִׁי
Y'SHa-aSHu NaFSHi,
y'SHHHa-aSHHHu nafSHHi.
You, God, You soothe, You soothe *my* soul.

Gentle, calm, intimate.
This isn't about the whole world,
it's about my world,
my soul, my essence.
I am: parent, friend, student, leader, shepherd, a rock.
I feel my Breath Within.
Each exhale, like wind scattering clouds,
releases a bit, of pain, worry, anger,
cools the raging fires of heart and head,
makes space for hope, joy, and gratitude.
I hear the sound *Shshshsh*,
and in the shining sun of this day,
my soul is soothed.

with each psalm on its day.

Thursday Week 3   *Psalm 81:11*

Open Your Mouth Wide

אָנֹכִי | יְיָ אֱלֹהֶיךָ הַמַּעַלְךָ מֵאֶרֶץ מִצְרָיִם
הַרְחֶב־פִּיךָ וַאֲמַלְאֵהוּ׃

I am Adonai your God
Who is bringing you up from the Land of Egypt;
Open wide your mouth and I shall fill it.

This is not about food.
No manna at dawn
or falling quails in the Sinai wilderness.
This is not about water.
No suddenly appearing well in the barren desert
or gushing stream from a stone cracked open.

It is a Psalmist's promise
of nourishment and hydration.
If I open my mouth, wide,
God will fill my heart and soul
with prayer, with praise,
with sounds and songs
I don't yet know,
with language I've never heard.

I pray before praying:
"Open my lips God,
that my mouth [will be filled] with praise and prayer."
I seek a secret password to release
the hidden door,
the stuck window,
the locked heart,
the broken soul.
Sometimes I offer the words by rote or without comprehension.
I sing and chant and even hum infinite melodies,

hoping one is the right key.
Sometimes the portal of prayer opens, sometimes not.

Once my mouth is open, wide, I can also be:
Broad-minded
Expansive of heart
Steady in my steps
Rooted to my ancestors
Sheltering to all
Shining with holiness
Open and free to choose life.

With the Psalmist I practice the promise:
With my mouth open, wide,
Your words flow like the songs of the birds at dawn—
each a hymn to the Creator,
each an expression of joy or longing,
or alarm or just an outpouring,
an overflowing, an offering,
sweet as honey,
the flavor of freedom.

with each psalm on its day.

Friday, Week 3   *Psalm 93:4*

The Guard

מְקֹלוֹת | מַיִם רַבִּים אַדִּירִים מִשְׁבְּרֵי־יָם אַדִּיר בַּמָּרוֹם יְיָ:
More powerful than their sound,
Than the crash of all the mighty breakers of the sea below,
Is the might on high of Adonai.

At Coast Guard Beach,
there are no guards
and there is a lot of coast.

The waves crash hard and fast onto each other.
Water and sand churn together,
brown, gold, gray, white.
The ocean pushes and pulls pebbles, stones—even boulders—
toward transformation.
The sea pops, bubbles, rolls, and rumbles,
unceasing on the shore.

At the edge of the turmoil
where the tide turns,
someone, some-ones, built a cairn.
Rocks beautifully balanced, one on another,
large on the bottom, smallest on top.
A game?
A sculpture?
An altar?
A message, to another made in God's image.
An offering,
to the sea, to the Creator, to our world.

There is no guard on this coast,
but there is
a prayer, a hope, an aspiration, a sign, a metaphor,
a gift with a message.

There is a Guard
who made this sand and sea.
Robed, not in a red bathing suit,
but in the sparkling light of the sun on the water.
Present from a place higher than a lifeguard stand.
With a call more compelling than a whistle.
On watch since time began.

The threat of drowning, of being swept away,
is real,
and we can balance like the rocks, the Rock.
The world churns at our feet.
The Life Guard is always present
on the coast, on high, everywhere,
and we stand firm too in this holy world.

with each psalm on its day.

Shabbat/Saturday, Week 3   *Psalm 92:10*

Wicked Like Weeds

כִּי הִנֵּה אֹיְבֶיךָ | יְיָ כִּי־הִנֵּה אֹיְבֶיךָ יֹאבֵדוּ
יִתְפָּרְדוּ כָּל־פֹּעֲלֵי אָוֶן:

For behold, Your foes, Adonai,
For behold, Your foes shall fall away—
All the workers of iniquity shall be scattered.

Sing and give thanks.
Share a story.
Play an instrument.
Appreciate joy and beauty,
and pause to praise the Wonder of the world.
Reflect on human limitations,
there is so much we don't understand, can't comprehend,
and yet we strive
for wisdom,
not wickedness.
Accept.
There are enemies in our lives,
many of them
at the very center,
as they are in this psalm.

What if we imagine our enemies with the Psalmist,
wicked like weeds.
Not foreign armies or domestic terrorists,
office bullies or nasty neighbors.
Instead:
destructive inclinations within us,
deep doubts,
harsh criticisms,
our insecurities,
addictions and abstentions, of all sorts.

They pop up, peep out, creep and crowd,
sprout and spread.
They can be:
stomped down,
plucked out,
managed if not mastered.
Enemies inevitably return,
and so do we,
to comprehend and confront them,
again
and again.

With Sacred Strength
we work
to subdue and scatter our adversaries.
With open eyes
we see them coming.
With listening ears
we hear their advance call.
With heads held high,
feet rooted like cedars,
we choose:
be just, noble, fruitful,
throughout life,
despite the enemies,
in spite of the enemies.

This too is a song of praise on a Sabbath day.

with each psalm on its day.

Week 4

Shmuel,
a gifted astronomer,
invited Chiya bar Rav (his dear friend's son)
to consider
the capacity of angels
to engage with sacred texts.

Each and every day God's angels are created.
They sing a psalm and immediately cease to exist.
But we humans are different.

We are created
new each day
and so too our songs/psalms.

Sunday, Week 4   *Psalm 24:7*

Honor at the Gate

שְׂאוּ שְׁעָרִים | רָאשֵׁיכֶם
וְהִנָּשְׂאוּ פִּתְחֵי עוֹלָם וְיָבוֹא מֶלֶךְ הַכָּבוֹד:

Raise up your heads, O regal gates—
Let yourselves be raised up, O doors to eternity!
Let there enter the Ruler of Glory!

I've known this Hebrew word all my life.
Melech: a king, the King.
Melech haolam, the King of the universe,
part of every blessing spoken.
As a child I learned,
a king is the partner to a queen.
In storybooks,
he sits on a throne and wears a crown.
In history texts, he is busy,
limiting freedoms of daughters,
choosing favored sons.
Is this the realm of the King of the universe,
of my prayer book?
No thanks.
No thrones,
no punishments,
no confined daughters for my God.

I learned a new word, when I began to study Hebrew
forty years ago, a biblical generation ago:
Kavod.
Kavod means: honor, respect for human dignity.
I later discovered *kavod* also means:
heavy physically or spiritually weighty.
This is not a surprising combination.

In Psalm 24, these two words come together,
five times in four verses,
and with them two worlds.
Melech HaKavod, a Ruler of Glory,
Ruler is better than King, for some,
but not for me.
I prefer Holy One of Glory,
but glory is hard to understand.
God is singular and unique, all-powerful,
with infinite names and uncountable attributes,
the weightiest of them all
Kavod.

Melech HaKavod . . .
The One Inside the Temple's Gates . . .
With the Psalmist we
push the gates open
to enter the portal of the heart
and sense the Holy of Holies.
With every breath,
each a new gateway,
we are in the presence of *Melech HaKavod*:
God Who Honors . . .
The Power of Respect . . .
Your Heavy Holiness . . .
Our Source of Dignity . . .
My Inspiration for Decency . . .
The responsibility is heavy,
but it is our honor,
to make *Melech HaKavod* manifest in the world.

with each psalm on its day.

Monday, Week 4   *Psalm 48:12*

Miriam's Story

יִשְׂמַח ׀ הַר־צִיּוֹן תָּגֵלְנָה בְּנוֹת יְהוּדֶה לְמַעַן מִשְׁפָּטֶיךָ:
Let Mount Zion rejoice,
Let the daughters of Judah be glad
Because of Your judgments.

Carefully concealed
in the most common translation as
"Let *b'not Y'hudah*, the *town* of Judah, rejoice,"
a woman tells her story,
of fear and faith, of celebration,
not accidentally
comparing terror and trembling to times of childbirth.

The Psalmist chose *b'not Y'hudah*, the daughters of Judah,
like *b'not Tz'lofchad*, the daughters of Zelophehad:
Mahlah, Noah, Hoglah, Milcah, and Tirzah.
Five courageous women whose voices were heard and who established
justice.
These daughters of Judah, with open eyes and open ears,
are the daughters of the daughters of the daughters of Miriam,
who led the women in dance at the shore of the sea.
With timbrels passed down through the generations,
they gather at the gates of Zion, the feminine name for Jerusalem,
and record their narrative for us.

Encircle *her*,
count *her* towers,
set your heart on *her* battlements,
walk among *her* palaces.

Imagine.
The women of Israel expanding the circle
down, around, through

her streets and gates.
Dancing with their daughter on the walls and across the rooftops.
Smiles wide, hands joined, voices raised
in praise to their God.
One circling energetic supportive community.
They sing their story, of phenomenal women,
long before Maya Angelou sang of the joy in her feet.
Music and melody long lost, their words endure in
the echo of sandals on stone,
the reflection of light on ramparts,
the grip of strong hands,
sweat and the sweet smiles,
the embodied memory of our people.
Rejoice in the tales of women, who together with God,
lead us,
throughout time and space.

Tuesday, Week 4   *Psalm 82:6*

Every One of You

אֲנִי־אָמַרְתִּי אֱלֹהִים אַתֶּם וּבְנֵי עֶלְיוֹן כֻּלְּכֶם:
I, God, have said: You are godlike beings,
And all of you are children of the Most High.

Before there were people
and before there was a Garden
there is water,
lots of water, all the same, everywhere.
On the third day of Creation,
God divides the primordial waters,
kulchem, every drop
into separate seas, and dry ground emerges.
Bounded by land,
fed by rivers,
frozen and carved into glaciers,
boiling and bubbling as geysers,
the waters wait.

Finally,
on the fifth day of Creation,
wings and fins take shape
swarms take flight,
creatures of the deep creep,
the seas fill with life
to become homes.

The waters, creations of the Most High,
are more like humans
than like their Creator.
They too can gasp for breath,
choke on plastic, perish.
Made to pulse with life,

they are waiting for us,
to judge what is right,
to rescue,
to redeem.

We finally arrive.
Creations of the Most High,
shaped from the dust of the earth,
animated by divine breath,
blood flowing with those original waters.
Every color.
Every size and ability.
Every age, gender, and economic status.
Every nationality.
Every belief in religion or politics.
All
creations of the Most High,
children of God,
Humans infused with Holiness,
like the first people in Eden.

Unlike roaring seas or dancing rivers,
we are responsible.
We are called to gather together,
to stand and speak and sing and work for justice.
Today is our day,
to return,
to begin, again, like Adam and Eve,
each of us,
all of us,
blessed to be
God's partners in the work of Creation.

Wednesday, Week 4 *Psalm 95:1–2*

An Invitation

לְכוּ נְרַנְּנָה לַיְיָ נָרִיעָה לְצוּר יִשְׁעֵנוּ׃
נְקַדְּמָה פָנָיו בְּתוֹדָה בִּזְמִרוֹת נָרִיעַ לוֹ׃

Come, let's sing to God!
Let's make a t'ruah *sound before the Rock of our deliverance!*
Let's walk thankfully into God's presence
With singing, with t'ruah *sounds,*
Meant just for You.

Who doesn't like to receive a personal invitation?
A formal embossed invitation to a wedding.
A text message to meet for coffee.
Some invitations we long to receive.
It can feel good to be welcomed, seen, needed,
appreciated for something that is uniquely ours
to bring to that exact moment.

This invitation is to holiness.
Come as we are,
with our imperfections and foibles.
Come with others
to do something we can do alone
but will improve exponentially
when done with solidarity,
even from a place of isolation—especially in a time of loneliness.

לְכוּ *L'chu.* Come on! Let's go!

נְרַנְּנָה *N'ran'nah.* Let's sing to God!
Let's sing
with eyes that see in the dark,
ears that hear in the silence,
mouths that open not with words of vengeance,
but with love and gratitude.

נָרִיעָה *Nariah*. Let's make *t'ruah* sounds, music!
Let's call to others
to come together,
to take action,
to turn ourselves and our world around.

לְצוּר יִשְׁעֵנוּ *L'tzur yisheinu*. Let's praise what endures!
Solid as Rock,
steady against storms,
a place where we can stand,
our God who delivers in large ways and small.

נְקַדְּמָה *N'kadmah*. Let's set out, walking!
Let's head to the east,
to the land of Abraham and Sarah,
faces raised in joy
as the sun rises.

בִּזְמִרוֹת *Biz'mirot*. Let's say yes
to an inviting God!
Let's lift our voices and open our hearts,
today,
without delay.

And once we've accepted the invitation,
let's extend it as well.
Come!
We call to friends, family,
those who are still strangers to us:
Come join us!
Sing with joy,
walk with gratitude,
accept the invitation of a Welcoming God,
enter the holiness of each day,
the sacred Shabbat,
where all are welcome.

> Psalm 95 is the first of the *Kabbalat Shabbat* psalms
> sung to welcome Shabbat each Friday evening.

with each psalm on its day.

Thursday, Week 4   *Psalm 81:13*

Stubborn Hearts

וָאֲשַׁלְּחֵהוּ בִּשְׁרִירוּת לִבָּם יֵלְכוּ בְּמוֹעֲצוֹתֵיהֶם׃

So I let them go in the stubbornness of their heart,
That they might walk according to their own counsels.

A stubborn heart.
This is not the hard heart of Pharaoh.
It is not the broken heart of the Psalmist.
It is not a closed heart or a heavy heart.
The same Hebrew letters used in the adjective "stubborn,"
spell the noun:
umbilical cord,
the flow of lifeblood between child and mother.
It is the word for
muscle or sinew,
the connections in the body we can strengthen,
train to remember.
It is the word for
a bracelet tied around the wrist,
a chain linked at the ankle.

This heart is connected but bound to the wrong place.
A heart that hears only its own pulse,
not the beat of another,
not the voice of the Creator.
This heart does not listen,
strays off course,
forgets mythic stories.
This heart of determination
turns in dogged pursuit
of false idols,
stories of the moment, money, or power,
rather than the Voice whose power can create.

We know this stubborn heart.
Small children, even grown adults
declare with feet stomping and fingers clenched into fists,
jaws locked into place and teeth gritted—
"I'll do it myself."
We use the muscle of this heart like a large motor skill,
trust breaks like wood,
love shatters like glass,
friendship tears like fabric.

The heart works best on its own,
finely honed small motor skills,
ready with every delicate breath.
A gentle soothing pulse for rest and sleep,
a strong steady beat for fear or joy.
So autonomic we forget.

Muscles can be strengthened
to do good
again.
Legs train to walk in God's ways.
Ears practice to listen more closely.
The stubborn heart connects
like the cord that binds parent to child,
to feed on sweet honey—
that flows to satisfy
from the Rock of Israel,
a place to stand.

with each psalm on its day.

Friday, Week 4　*Psalm 93:5*

Curtains for the House

נֶאֶמְנוּ מְאֹד לְבֵיתְךָ נַאֲוָה־קֹדֶשׁ יְיָ לְאֹרֶךְ יָמִים: | עֵדֹתֶיךָ

Your testimonies are very faithful.
Holy beauty will curtain Your house,
Adonai,
For long days,
Long, long days.

God,
God's world,
and God's house
all robed and wrapped,
draped in nobility, strength, in holy beauty,
as on a first day of spring,

Teeny tiny brown buds turn pale green,
minuscule leaves emerge, verdant, vibrant, vibrating.
Brilliant purple, deep orange, shining white crocuses
pop up from their blankets of soil and pine needles,
petals open to the gentle rain.

Hosts—of golden daffodils—
rise sturdy on their stems,
each on its own schedule.
A few sleep late,
wrapped tightly in light-brown blankets.
The early risers wake,
open and stretch their petals
to catch the sun's light.
The wind blows and they bow, as if in prayer:
singing with their hearts raised,
open to all the universe brings,
sun and storm.

With strong roots and flexible stems, they thrive,
for a day, for a week,
some for more than a month,
rooted in the ground.
Radiant in a vase,
the cleanest shades of yellow,
each a herald to the solstice
chasing darkness from the world,
stretching light like a tent cloth.

I crouch
like a crocus,
my basket empty,
waiting for sustenance.

I stand tall
like the daffodils,
confident in the crowd,
swaying, bending, with an open heart.

I shine
my fragile light among the robes and curtains,
illuminating inspiration in God's firmly established world,

I dwell
among the flowers of the spring,
the annuals,
bulbs planted long ago
and nearly forgotten beneath the earth,
holy beauty in God's house,
a curtain, a carpet,
for long long days.

with each psalm on its day.

Shabbat/Saturday, Week 4   *Psalm 92:14–15*

It's Easy Being Green

שְׁתוּלִים בְּבֵית יְיָ בְּחַצְרוֹת אֱלֹהֵינוּ יַפְרִיחוּ׃
עוֹד יְנוּבוּן בְּשֵׂיבָה דְּשֵׁנִים וְרַעֲנַנִּים יִהְיוּ׃

Planted in the House of Adonai,
they will sprout nobly in the courts of our God.
They shall be fruitful even in old age,
Green and luxuriant shall they be.

My once parched concrete courtyard is now verdant.
All year, every day, plants grow and change.
Pale pink azalea blossoms pop open in the shade.
Chive sprouts grow tall before they bend over.
Parsley perks up as its roots fill with water.
A second tiny fig begins to ripen.
The red geranium stretches toward the sun.
Local grasses turn from brown to green after the rain.
A new yellow hibiscus flower blooms wide,
at the same time each day,
and withers as the sun sets.
Growing and greening each day:
a wonder to behold the infinite varieties of species,
a miracle to witness each tiny transformation,
a blessing to see in the garden's diverse shapes and colors,
Creativity.

The sprouting vegetation, seed-bearing plants,
fruit trees of all sorts bearing fruit with the seed in it,
do what their ancestors did in Eden,
right here in this courtyard of *Adonai.*
They make it look easy to be green.
But sprouting like a palm,
standing tall like a cedar,

establishing roots,
standing in the presence of Holiness,
is not easy for plants
or people.
Plants never stop their work,
but we humans, like God in the Garden,
we stop on Shabbat.
And when we do,
we notice,
like the plants,
we too are nourished with rain in its seasons.

God's blessings to us pour out:
breath, Torah, mitzvot, each other.
With them we thrive and strive,
to grow and live upright,
aware we are not God—
in us, imperfection abounds and abides.
We sing
to the Rock, who creates and nurtures.
It is good, very good, to give thanks to God.

Rosh Chodesh

Rabbi Mordechai Yosef of Izbitza,
at a dark time,
understood
holiness shines in multiple dimensions.

The Divine shines:
in the world of daily life
in the cycle of the year
in the opening of the soul.

Each month's moon is an invitation:
to glimpse
the One Light of Holiness
in this place, at this time, with our heart.
We too wax and wane,
even as we are
new each day.

Psalm 104 for Rosh Chodesh

1 Praise Adonai, O my being,
Adonai my God, You are grand indeed!
You are clothed in surpassing splendor—
　　2 Wrapping Yourself in light like a cloak,
　　Unwrapping the heavens like a curtain of
　　　　smoke,
　　3 Laying the beams of Your upper chambers
　　　　in the waters,
　　Turning clouds into Your chariot,
　　Walking about on the wings of the wind,
　　4 Making the winds Your messengers;
　　Flaming fire, Your ministers.

5 You have established earth on her foundations—
It shall not totter, to infinity and beyond.
6 You covered it with the deep like a mantle—
The waters stood up on the mountains.
　　7 They ran away from Your rebuke,
　　They hurried off from the sound of Your
　　　　thunder.
　　8 Mountains rose up, valleys dropped down
　　To the very place You had established for them.
　　9 You set up a boundary they could not cross,
　　So they could not roar back to deluge the earth.

　　10 You are the One who sends forth streams
　　　　into the river valleys
　　That meander among the mountains;
　　11 They give water to every beast of the field;
　　The wild donkeys quench their thirst.
　　12 Above them hover the heavenly flocks,
　　From among the foliage they send forth their
　　　　voice.

תהילים פרק 104

1 בָּרְכִי נַפְשִׁי אֶת־יְיָ
יְיָ אֱלֹהַי גָּדַלְתָּ מְּאֹד
הוֹד וְהָדָר לָבָשְׁתָּ:
2 עֹטֶה־אוֹר כַּשַּׂלְמָה
נוֹטֶה שָׁמַיִם כַּיְרִיעָה:
3 הַמְקָרֶה בַמַּיִם עֲלִיּוֹתָיו
הַשָּׂם־עָבִים רְכוּבוֹ
הַמְהַלֵּךְ עַל־כַּנְפֵי־רוּחַ:
4 עֹשֶׂה מַלְאָכָיו רוּחוֹת
מְשָׁרְתָיו אֵשׁ לֹהֵט:

5 יָסַד־אֶרֶץ עַל־מְכוֹנֶיהָ
בַּל־תִּמּוֹט עוֹלָם וָעֶד:
6 תְּהוֹם כַּלְּבוּשׁ כִּסִּיתוֹ
עַל־הָרִים יַעַמְדוּ מָיִם:
7 מִן־גַּעֲרָתְךָ יְנוּסוּן
מִן־קוֹל רַעַמְךָ יֵחָפֵזוּן:
8 יַעֲלוּ הָרִים יֵרְדוּ בְקָעוֹת
אֶל־מְקוֹם זֶה | יָסַדְתָּ לָהֶם:
9 גְּבוּל־שַׂמְתָּ בַּל־יַעֲבֹרוּן
בַּל־יְשֻׁבוּן לְכַסּוֹת הָאָרֶץ:

10 הַמְשַׁלֵּחַ מַעְיָנִים בַּנְּחָלִים
בֵּין הָרִים יְהַלֵּכוּן:
11 יַשְׁקוּ כָּל־חַיְתוֹ שָׂדָי
יִשְׁבְּרוּ פְרָאִים צְמָאָם:
12 עֲלֵיהֶם עוֹף־הַשָּׁמַיִם יִשְׁכּוֹן
מִבֵּין עֳפָאיִם יִתְּנוּ־קוֹל:

13 You water the hills from Your upper chamber;
From the fruit of Your works the earth is satisfied.
14 You make grass sprout up for the cattle,
Herbage for the work of the human world
To bring forth bread from the earth,

   15 Wine that rejoices the human heart,
   Making the face glow brighter than oil,
   And bread—sustaining the human heart.
   16 The trees of Adonai drink their fill,
   The cedars of Lebanon which God has
      planted,
   17 Where birds build nests:
   The stork's house is in the fir trees.
   18 The crags are for the mountain goats,
   The rocks are a refuge for rabbits.
   19 God made a moon for seasons;
   The sun knows the time to go in.
   20 You decree darkness—and it is night,
   When all the creatures of the forest crawl
      about,
   21 The young lions roar for their carrion,
   And seek their food from God.
   22 The sun rises—they withdraw,
   And spread out in their lairs.

   23 Human beings go forth to their work,
   To their labor, until evening.

24 How many are Your works, Adonai!
All of them You made with wisdom!
The earth is full of Your creatures.

   25 This is the sea—great and many hands wide!
   There—creeping things without number,
   Wild things, little ones and big ones.

13 מַשְׁקֶה הָרִים מֵעֲלִיּוֹתָיו
מִפְּרִי מַעֲשֶׂיךָ תִּשְׂבַּע הָאָרֶץ:
14 מַצְמִיחַ חָצִיר | לַבְּהֵמָה
וְעֵשֶׂב לַעֲבֹדַת הָאָדָם
לְהוֹצִיא לֶחֶם מִן־הָאָרֶץ:
15 וְיַיִן | יְשַׂמַּח לְבַב־אֱנוֹשׁ
לְהַצְהִיל פָּנִים מִשָּׁמֶן
וְלֶחֶם לְבַב־אֱנוֹשׁ יִסְעָד:
16 יִשְׂבְּעוּ עֲצֵי יְיָ
אַרְזֵי לְבָנוֹן אֲשֶׁר נָטָע:
17 אֲשֶׁר־שָׁם צִפֳּרִים יְקַנֵּנוּ
חֲסִידָה בְּרוֹשִׁים בֵּיתָהּ:
18 הָרִים הַגְּבֹהִים לַיְּעֵלִים
סְלָעִים מַחְסֶה לַשְׁפַנִּים:
19 עָשָׂה יָרֵחַ לְמוֹעֲדִים
שֶׁמֶשׁ יָדַע מְבוֹאוֹ:
20 תָּשֶׁת־חֹשֶׁךְ וִיהִי לָיְלָה
בּוֹ־תִרְמֹשׂ כָּל־חַיְתוֹ־יָעַר:
21 הַכְּפִירִים שֹׁאֲגִים לַטָּרֶף
וּלְבַקֵּשׁ מֵאֵל אָכְלָם:
22 תִּזְרַח הַשֶּׁמֶשׁ יֵאָסֵפוּן
וְאֶל־מְעוֹנֹתָם יִרְבָּצוּן:

23 יֵצֵא אָדָם לְפָעֳלוֹ
וְלַעֲבֹדָתוֹ עֲדֵי־עָרֶב:

24 מָה־רַבּוּ מַעֲשֶׂיךָ | יְיָ
כֻּלָּם בְּחָכְמָה עָשִׂיתָ
מָלְאָה הָאָרֶץ קִנְיָנֶךָ:

25 זֶה | הַיָּם גָּדוֹל וּרְחַב יָדָיִם
שָׁם־רֶמֶשׂ וְאֵין מִסְפָּר
חַיּוֹת קְטַנּוֹת עִם־גְּדֹלוֹת:

26 There go the ships,
And Leviathan, this creature You formed to
    play in the sea—

27 All of them wait for You
To give them their food in its time.
28 You give to them, they go gathering,
You open Your hand—they are given good
    aplenty.

29 You hide Your face, they are terrified,
You cut off their breath—they perish,
And to their dust they return.
30 You send forth Your breath, they are created
    anew
And You renew the face of the ground.

31 Let the glory of Adonai last forever,
Let Adonai rejoice in divine works,
32 Who looks upon the earth and it trembles,
Who touches the mountains and they smoke.

33 Let me sing to Adonai during my lifetime,
Let me sing praise to God while I still am!
34 Let my meditation rest sweetly upon the
    Holy One—
I will rejoice in Adonai!
35 Let sinners cease from the earth
And wicked people be no more;
Praise Adonai, O my being,
Hall'lu-Yah, Praise Adonai!

26 שָׁם אֳנִיּוֹת יְהַלֵּכוּן
לִוְיָתָן זֶה־יָצַרְתָּ לְשַׂחֶק־בּוֹ:

27 כֻּלָּם אֵלֶיךָ יְשַׂבֵּרוּן
לָתֵת אָכְלָם בְּעִתּוֹ:
28 תִּתֵּן לָהֶם יִלְקֹטוּן
תִּפְתַּח יָדְךָ יִשְׂבְּעוּן טוֹב:

29 תַּסְתִּיר פָּנֶיךָ יִבָּהֵלוּן
תֹּסֵף רוּחָם יִגְוָעוּן
וְאֶל־עֲפָרָם יְשׁוּבוּן:
30 תְּשַׁלַּח רוּחֲךָ יִבָּרֵאוּן
וּתְחַדֵּשׁ פְּנֵי אֲדָמָה:

31 יְהִי כְבוֹד יְיָ לְעוֹלָם
יִשְׂמַח יְיָ בְּמַעֲשָׂיו:
32 הַמַּבִּיט לָאָרֶץ וַתִּרְעָד
יִגַּע בֶּהָרִים וְיֶעֱשָׁנוּ:

33 אָשִׁירָה לַיְיָ בְּחַיָּי
אֲזַמְּרָה לֵאלֹהַי בְּעוֹדִי:
34 יֶעֱרַב עָלָיו שִׂיחִי
אָנֹכִי אֶשְׂמַח בַּיְיָ:
35 יִתַּמּוּ חַטָּאִים | מִן־הָאָרֶץ
וּרְשָׁעִים | עוֹד אֵינָם
בָּרְכִי נַפְשִׁי אֶת־יְיָ הַלְלוּ־יָהּ:

Rosh Chodesh Tishrei　　*Psalm 104:30*

Prayers for the Path

תְּשַׁלַּח רוּחֲךָ יִבָּרֵאוּן וּתְחַדֵּשׁ פְּנֵי אֲדָמָה׃

You send forth Your breath, they are created anew
And You renew the face of the ground.

Tishrei takes patience and pacing
to persevere and prevail,
and the Psalmist knew this precious path,
and the words of prayer.

תְחַדֵּשׁ *T'chadeish* . . . renew.
Rosh Chodesh Tishrei
is Rosh HaShanah,
the start of the year in the seventh month,
the birthday of the world,
proclaimed by the sound of the shofar.
Ready,
I pray with the Psalmist,
trembling on a mountain, as the rivers roar around me,
from the darkness there will be light,
when I turn
toward wholeness,
repair, myself, our world.

תְּשַׁלַּח רוּחֲךָ *Tishalach ruchacha* . . . send [back] Your breath.
Yom Kippur is
the tenth of Tishrei,
a day to imagine death
and give thanks for resurrecting Breath.
Rebirthed,
like the Psalmist,
I pray with an open heart—

may my sins
be cast away
and forgiveness and compassion reign.

פְּנֵי אֲדָמָה *P'nei adamah* . . . the face of the earth.
Sukkot is
under the full moon,
the face of the earth glows,
rich with the human harvest,
human faces too,
shaped from *adamah*, earth,
infinitely varied, gathering as one
raising the fallen sukkah.
Rejoicing,
I pray with the Psalmist,
in the face of fragility,
for a shelter of peace over our world.

יְבָּרֵאוּן *Yibarei-un* . . . they are created.
Sh'mini Atzeret–Simchat Torah is
a time of tarrying.
Barely a breath between,
the end of the Torah
and back to the beginning,
b'reishit bara Elohim,
God creates it all, always.
Death and life,
the instant between,
and the choice in our hands.
Revived,
I pray with the Psalmist,
lingering with voice raised,
satiated by what is given,
satisfied with what I've gathered.

With all my soul I bless You, *Adonai*,
Hallelujah.

Psalm 104 for Rosh Chodesh, the new month, begins on page 110.

with each psalm on its day.

Rosh Chodesh Cheshvan   *Psalm 104:23*

Simple and Sweet

יֵצֵא אָדָם לְפָעֳלוֹ וְלַעֲבֹדָתוֹ עֲדֵי־עָרֶב:
Human beings go forth to their work,
To their labor, until evening.

Some call it Mar-Cheshvan,
the bitter month of Cheshvan,
but not me.
Tishrei is super sweet—
apple cake with cinnamon,
pomegranate's juice,
etrog boiled with sugar into preserves when Sukkot concludes,
Torah, sweet as honey
dripping from the bottle opened on Simchat Torah,
to make the learning a delight.

Cheshvan is more simple.
No complicated recipes,
less sticky mess in the kitchen, less stickiness in life.
The moon rises, low and wide, a satisfied smile.
There was work well done, prayer, *tzedakah*, repentance,
since the last new moon.
Cheshvan is wide open,
until Sigd arrives,
twenty-eight spacious days for the labor of the sacred heart
to become holy work of the hands,
sustenance to savor in the mouth for a month.

"Human beings go forth to their *work*,
to their *labor* until evening."
Po-al, the daily grind kind of work,
providing food and clothing and shelter.
Avodah, related to the ancient sacrifices of flock and field,

today's labor of prayer and acts of justice.
We taste them both,
an entire month to integrate the dual aspects of our lives
and turn new commitments into practices.

Sugar alone won't nourish us.
On the seventh day of this month we pray,
"Send rain, gentle rain and wind to nurture my seeds."
It's a prayer for the Land of Israel, the world, and each of us
for the blessing of rain,
which brings, slowly, new growth.

In four wide-open weeks,
while the light of the sun wanes,
the brightness of possibility prevails.
The rain from the sky,
the salty tears of the eyes,
the sweet work of the hands,
the transforming labor of the heart,
combine in miraculous alchemy.
In the earth,
and in the body formed of earth,
deep within,
where only the soul sees:
seeds rest,
energy builds,
roots take hold,
hope thrives.
In the sweet pause of time,
something new and nourishing prepares,
and we wait,
savoring the sacred space.

Psalm 104 for Rosh Chodesh, the new month, begins on page 110.

with each psalm on its day.

Rosh Chodesh Kislev   *Psalm 104:4*

A Message in Each Light

עֹשֶׂה מַלְאָכָיו רוּחוֹת מְשָׁרְתָיו אֵשׁ לֹהֵט:
Making the winds Your messengers;
Flaming fire, Your ministers.

The flaming fire [each tiny flame of the Chanukah menorah]
You make Your messenger.

Each flame is kindled by human hands:
not unfurled across the heavens like Your stars,
not spanning the sky like Your sun,
not steady in its seasons like Your moon.
A sacred human obligation to set them and kindle them,
not to use them, only to behold them,
ever increasing, united and unique.

Each flame, a minister from You:
each messenger, on a mission from Light itself.
Emerging when the sun is not present,
in dreams, on the road, at birth and death, every Shabbat,
on eight nights of Chanukah.
Each angel of fire delivers a unique gift.

One tiny message the first night.
And then two more on the second.
And on and on it goes, eight nights of light.
Thirty-six individual guests,
each one bearing a different offering
to each one who offers blessing.
Twice eighteen, for life . . .
Barchi nafshi, the psalm begins.
I bless with the essence of my life,
the spark breathes,
Light emerges from darkness.

. . . to remember, to thank, to praise

Barchi nafshi, the psalm concludes.
I bless with the essence of my life,
my soul breathes,
Light grows, nourished with hope.

Remember with this light:
sing, pray, praise, rejoice, be still,
and give thanks
for all God's miracles and mighty acts.

Psalm 104 for Rosh Chodesh, the new month, begins on page 110.

Psalm 30 is read each day of Chanukah in addition to the Psalm of the Day. This psalm was selected because its opening phrase, "a [re]dedication song for the house of David," connects to the victory of the Maccabees. It is a perfect choice as it expresses both the dark depth of our despair and our abiding anticipation of returning to the light.

with each psalm on its day.

Rosh Chodesh Tevet   *Psalm 104:29*

Hidden Hope

תַּסְתִּיר פָּנֶיךָ יִבָּהֵלוּן תֹּסֵף רוּחָם יִגְוָעוּן וְאֶל־עֲפָרָם יְשׁוּבוּן׃

You hide Your face, they are terrified,
You cut off their breath—they perish,
And to their dust they return.

Chanukah is the only Jewish holiday spanning two months.
Eight nights of lights,
the twenty-fifth of Kislev through the second of Tevet.

Tu BiSh'vat has a singular name and date,
the fifteenth of Sh'vat.

Purim turns it all upside down.
Walled cities celebrate on the fifteenth,
unwalled villages on the fourteenth,
but always in Adar,
except of course when there's a leap month
and it's in Adar II.

Pesach is simple.
"Eat no leavened bread for seven days"
beginning when the moon is full on the fifteenth of Nisan.
The moon on the wane but still visible when the festival concludes.

Sukkot is similar.
"Dwell in booths for seven days," under the full moon, day fifteen to
twenty-one of Tishrei.

Chanukah is different.
The sky is dark and grows darker as the candles increase.
Psalm 30 gives voice to the human fear as
the Night Light vanishes,
"You hide Your face and I am terrified."
We dread the dark of Kislev

and await the arrival of Tevet.
We watch and wait,
like a patient waiting for a doctor's call,
for a tiny smiling sliver of light
in the year's longest night sky.
Slim and low on the right side,
the new moon resembles the Hebrew letter *reish*.
ר–*Reish*, for the start of Rosh Chodesh.

We can read the richness of this *reish*:
Ramah and *rom'mu*, for the peaks and the praise,
Rinah, joy-filled song.
Ratzon, God's will and pleasure blessing us.
Ruach, divine breath and human soul.
R'fuah, the healing of souls and bodies, of our world.

All this feels hidden in the dark, like God's face,
and we are terrified.
But we are alive, maybe mired in mud,
but not sunk into the pit.

Tevet is a light shining with hope.
We are renewed,
over and over again, not only when we die,
but while we breathe.
The eight lights of Chanukah blaze bright before they flicker out.
The moon rises, and we affirm
we live in the Light,
singing, praising, crying, praying,
blessing with all our breath—Hallelujah!

Psalm 104 for Rosh Chodesh, the new month, begins on page 110.
Psalm 30 is read each day of Chanukah in addition to the
  Psalm of the Day.
Psalm 30:8 uses the same language of God's hidden face and
  our fear at this time of year:
יְיָ בִּרְצוֹנְךָ הֶעֱמַדְתָּה לְהַרְרִי־עֹז הִסְתַּרְתָּ פָנֶיךָ הָיִיתִי נִבְהָל:
Adonai, it pleased You to establish a stronghold on my mountain.
Then You hid Your face—I was terrified!

with each psalm on its day.

Rosh Chodesh Sh'vat   *Psalm 104:16–17*

Holy Ways

יִשְׂבְּעוּ עֲצֵי יְיָ אַרְזֵי לְבָנוֹן אֲשֶׁר נָטָע:
אֲשֶׁר־שָׁם צִפֳּרִים יְקַנֵּנוּ חֲסִידָה בְּרוֹשִׁים בֵּיתָהּ:

The trees of Adonai drink their fill,
The cedars of Lebanon which God has planted,
Where birds build nests:
The stork's house is in the fir trees.

Cedar grows straight and tall.
Fir and cypress welcome nesting in their branches.
Willow shades the riverbank.
Saguaro cluster in a parched desert.
Aspen quake on the mountain's side.
Pine thrives on the rise of the salt marsh.
Redwood ages in a dappled and dense grove.
Maple shines in the sun-drenched yard.
Pomegranate bursts with crimson crowns.
Live oak stands steady as squirrels leap.
Pecan on the corner is laden with nuts.

Ever since the third day of Creation,
all the trees planted in the House of God
have been holding on to the old holy ways.
As if at prayer, they sway and bend, and stand again, in the wind.
They sink roots, shallow and wide, deep and winding.
They drink their fill and welcome nests.
They offer fruit and seed for the future.
They work together, holding on
to the ways of *Atikah*—the Ancient One of Old.

In Sh'vat, the almond holds on too.
It is still deep winter in some places,
midsummer in others,

but on the hillside
along the historic road from Tel Aviv to Jerusalem,
God's Courtyard for generations,
photosynthesis is busy in the branches
producing holiness.
On Tu BiSh'vat, the New Year for Trees,
eager to share its beauty, offer its hospitality, bring forth fruit,
the almond tree blooms.
White and pink flowers glow,
even in the dark.
With each cell of its root system, it sends a message:
I'm here. I'm here to help.
The ancient message transmitted to the trees,
and to us.

Hold on to the ancient ways,
do what you were made to do:
give thanks to God,
with all your soul sing praise,
Hallelujah!

Psalm 104 for Rosh Chodesh, the new month, begins on page 110.

"The trees, the trees, just holding on
to the old, holy ways." (Mary Oliver)

Rosh Chodesh Adar   *Psalm 104:34*

The Moon Smiles

יֶעֱרַב עָלָיו שִׂיחִי אָנֹכִי אֶשְׂמַח בַּיְיָ:

Let my meditation rest sweetly upon the Holy One—
I will rejoice in Adonai!

The night is dark,
the air is cold,
the sky is clear,
and low on the western horizon,
and just above the canopy of the trees—
the moon smiles.
The heavens rejoice as Adar begins with its historic promise,
"Whoever enters Adar increases in joy"—
a celestial message for the month to come.

The moon marks this season with an unabashed grin,
to announce the inside-out joy of Purim,
off-balance near the center of Adar.
On the fourteenth day of the month,
tell a timeless tale of
courage,
bravery,
beauty,
intellect;
accompanied by
fear,
deceit,
vengeance,
violence.

It's dark, but it's Adar.
Be happy, says the moon.
I try.

As surely as birds make their nests,
and springs flow downhill,
humans reflect
on the Holy One who made it all,
and rejoice
in the light of the Luminary in the Heavens.

This is the Light,
of Esther, Vashti, and Mordechai,
the gladness, happiness, and honor
that fills homes.
Their light shines still when people
speak truth to power,
stand and walk and speak and act
for what is right and just and respectful
of all Creation.
God rejoices in all that the Divine has done,
perfect and imperfect,
beautiful and broken,
and so can I.

Psalm 104 for Rosh Chodesh, the new month, begins on page 110.

Note: On years when there is Adar I and Adar II, either use this Reflection for Focus for both months or use a weekday Reflection for Focus. See page xxxi for more details.

with each psalm on its day.

Rosh Chodesh Nisan   *Psalm 104:4*

Your Messenger

עֹשֶׂה מַלְאָכָיו רוּחוֹת מְשָׁרְתָיו אֵשׁ לֹהֵט:
Making the winds Your messengers;
Flaming fire, Your ministers.

A cold gust blows the branches of the bare trees,
they scrape against one another.
Your message:
Take shelter,
use your roots for balance,
for sustenance in every storm.

A warm steady breeze crosses the marsh,
the tide silently glides out, and the grasses rise from the mud.
Your message:
Look closely, listen carefully, outside
and inside,
the house, the office, the heart.

The lightest of winds, young and new, hovers close to the ground.
Adjusting the poses of the not-yet-bloomed buds.
Your message:
Learn and practice—
what is soft and small can also be
strong, soothing, sustaining.

Once,
Your strong east wind blew all night and turned the sea into dry
ground,
a messenger of redemption to Your people, all people,
leading them toward freedom,
breaking them out from the brickmaking of racism,
the forced labor of labels, the bonds of prison cells,
the enslavement of callousness and hate.

. . . to remember, to thank, to praise

It was a message so essential and enduring,
the Messenger needed help.
Miriam was there,
song ready, timbrel in hand, heart full of faith.
She knew,
the divine breath You breathed into each set of human lungs
makes all of us Your messengers—
there would be reason to celebrate.

The winds outside and inside
carry Your message in the month of Nisan.
I prepare for Pesach,
rejoicing in every generation
as the moon rises full in the spring,
what was and what could be.
Like Your wind
in the trees, on the marsh, around the garden, at the sea:
I embrace my mission,
with words and songs, hearts and hands,
as I celebrate Your gift of freedom
and deliver Your message to our world.

Psalm 104 for Rosh Chodesh, the new month, begins on page 110.

with each psalm on its day.

Rosh Chodesh Iyar   *Psalm 104:10*

Streams of Healing

הַמְשַׁלֵּחַ מַעְיָנִים בַּנְּחָלִים בֵּין הָרִים יְהַלֵּכוּן:
*You are the One who sends forth streams
   into river valleys
That meander among the mountains.*

The month of Iyar is spelled in Hebrew
א-י-י-ר
alef, yod, yod, reish,
a secret code to open the ancient story of the season.

The sea crossing is behind them.
The epic song sung,
the joyous dance with drums concluded.
They huddle together, just across the border,
images still vivid in the mind,
sounds of struggling horses echoing in the ears,
the loss of meager slavery possessions a deep sadness.
The sun is hot,
the children are hungry,
the water is bitter.
The source of life,
like the blood-filled Nile of their lived nightmare,
is not fit for drinking.

How can it be?
How can the suffering continue on this side of the sea?
How can a person, a people,
heal from such trauma, find sweetness again,
in *Marah*, the Bitter Place?

You have to know the code.
Alef, yod, yod, reish.
א *Alef=Ani,* I AM

י *Yod, Yod* = (combine to spell the name of God) ADONAI
ר *Reish* = *Rofecha*, YOUR HEALER
The letters spell the month of Iyar,
they are words of promise—hope—for the generations.

Every Iyar, Jeremiah teaches us, again,
to use the code, to heal the enduring trauma.
He reintroduces *Mikveih Yisrael*,
Hope of Israel,
All-Embracing Waters,
Healing Place.
We seem to stutter as we speak the ancient words,
"Heal me, *Adonai*, let me be healed."
The Psalmist also knows the healing code of Iyar.

Healer, You are Always the One,
who sends the streams to:
quench thirst with water,
soothe souls with sound,
nourish all life with blessing.

Your water, infused with the essence of Creation,
falls from above, bubbles from below, flows in all directions,
until all are satisfied.
Enough to heal what ails the world:
prescriptions for the plagues of incivility, inequity, and injustice,
balms for broken bodies,
stitches for torn hearts,
breath from the beginning, to clear muddled minds.

There will always be trauma,
and there is always Iyar,
so there can always be healing.
A gift from the Well,
flowing in streams and among mountains,
sweetening our lives,
healing our world.

Psalm 104 for Rosh Chodesh, the new month, begins on page 110.

with each psalm on its day.

Rosh Chodesh Sivan   *Psalm 104:15*

Knead Words of Torah

> וְיַיִן ׀ יְשַׂמַּח לְבַב־אֱנוֹשׁ לְהַצְהִיל פָּנִים מִשָּׁמֶן
> וְלֶחֶם לְבַב־אֱנוֹשׁ יִסְעָד:
>
> *Wine that rejoices the human heart,*
> *Making the face glow brighter than oil,*
> *And bread—sustaining the human heart.*

In Sivan we finally arrive at the mountain.
From the edge of the sea in Nisan
through the open wilderness of Iyar,
we retrace the steps each year.
The soul of a slave wanders,
moving from servitude to Pharaoh
toward service to God.
Now the body of the hungry waits,
praying for a new Source of Sustenance.

In perfect balance,
rain and sun
bring forth food,
seeds sown transform to harvest.
God's gift into our hands,
bread from the earth.

At Sinai, after forty-nine days of counting,
seven weeks of seven days,
from the day after Passover to the day before Shavuot,
we embrace a new kind of nourishment.
Another inspired gift to us,
Torah.
Words, like grain,
sustain bodies and fuel imaginations.
Family stories,

with flawed ancestors and inspirational characters,
fill the mind with memories and motivation.
Mitzvot, ethical obligations and ritual responsibilities,
timebound and timeless,
compel us, choose life and blessing,
for ourselves and others.

There are enough letters in the sacred scroll
to feed the whole world,
to nourish peace,
here and now and forever.
Like bread we bake with God's grain to sustain the body,
we knead words of Torah,
wait for the verses to rise from the page,
bake them into our minds,
share them with others.
Our sacred story is the bread,
sustaining the human heart.

The Torah we receive, over and over again,
doesn't come easily,
sprouting like grass for cattle.
We are always numbering our days,
making them count,
navigating a wilderness toward wisdom.
We are continually
between the narrow places of Egypt
and the open expanse of Sinai,
between servitude to our work
and the service of holiness.
We remember,
wine may bring joy
but our bread,
words of Torah,
sustain the heart.

Psalm 104 for Rosh Chodesh, the new month, begins on page 110.

with each psalm on its day.

Rosh Chodesh Tammuz   *Psalm 104:19*

Me and My Shadow

עָשָׂה יָרֵחַ לְמוֹעֲדִים שֶׁמֶשׁ יָדַע מְבוֹאוֹ:

God made a moon for seasons;
The sun knows the time to go in.

My shadow is loyal.
It mirrors my steps on the sidewalk,
my stance in the sand.
It distorts my image,
smooths the rough edges,
disguises the details.
With my shadow I am never alone,
God's light is always with me.

Except in Tammuz,
on the solstice,
when the sun is at its peak,
when the day (in the Northern Hemisphere)
is filled with heat,
and so much light,
even shadows take shelter.

My instinct too
is to hide.
It's too hot, too bright, too intense
without my shadow,
the Ever-Present Light
that is always
beside me, behind me, before me.
But then my eyes adjust.
It seems the sun stands still,
and I wonder,
does it really know the time to go in?

Slowly I see,
with courage like Joshua,
as the sun hung in the sky above for a full day.
His battle was real by the walls of Jericho,
and in Tammuz mine are real too:
an ever-growing ego and guilty conscience,
greedy desires and selfish inclinations.

I yearn to be like Betzalel,
skilled craftsman of the desert Tabernacle,
whose name affirms, I am "in the shadow of God," always.
Maybe the sun *does* know the time to go in,
and it is now.

The Light finds a home:
a tiny space for a glowing spark to dwell,
in my *Mishkan*,
the holy place that is my body,
my life.
It's good the sun knows its way
since I don't always know mine.
In the brightness of Tammuz I see,
secure,
even without my shadow,
I bless the Creator of Light.

הַמְּאִירָה לָאָרֶץ וְלַדָּרִים עָלֶיהָ
בְּרַחֲמִים וּבְטוּבָה
מְחַדֶּשֶׁת בְּכָל־יוֹם תָּמִיד
מַעֲשֵׂה בְרֵאשִׁית:

The Illuminator lights up the world
and all of her inhabitants with mercy,
and in Her goodness,
each day renews
the act of creation.

Psalm 104 for Rosh Chodesh, the new month, begins on page 110.

with each psalm on its day.

Rosh Chodesh Av   *Psalm 104:5*

Unshaken but Stirred

יָסַד־אֶרֶץ עַל־מְכוֹנֶיהָ בַּל־תִּמּוֹט עוֹלָם וָעֶד:
You have established earth on her foundations—
It shall not totter, to infinity and beyond.

Av is a month
for sitting, weeping, remembering.
Across millennia and miles,
calamities collide on the Ninth of Av,
failures of compassion and chaos flood the earth,
threaten destruction of Creation.

Someplace in the Sinai wilderness, upon the scouts' return: Doubt.
Jerusalem, 586 BCE and 70 CE: Destruction.
England, 1290: Deportation.
Spain, 1492: Forced Conversion.
Warsaw, 1942: Genocide.
Nagasaki, 1945: Nuclear Bombing.
Anywhere, anytime: Any pain of body or soul afflicting anyone.
Always, a cry from deep within,
a question without an answer: *Eichah*, how?

I know the ancient lament:
I cry those tears.
My heart is a tumult
of anxiety, loneliness, frustration, disappointment, self-doubt.
My soul melts in the sun's blaze of summer,
huddled and hidden, deep in the darkness of daylight.

אֵיכָה *Eichah* . . . How did this happen to me?
אֵיכָה *Eichah* . . . How did this happen to those I love?
אֵיכָה *Eichah* . . . How did this happen to our world?

I shake in my core.
But the earth remains,

. . . to remember, to thank, to praise

steady in its orbit.
I voice the affirmation
that stirs me to care, to act, to live.
A reminder each month,
and Av's promise to Elul:
The mountains may tremble, and the hills shake
but God's *chesed*, generous love, never leaves us
and God's *b'rit shalom*, covenant of wholeness, lasts forever . . .

It's a month before the last month of the year.
All I haven't done,
all I did do that I shouldn't have done,
begins to rise.
I *am* shaken, awake.
The words rouse me
to turn and return.
Dry the tears and calm the heart,
restore shape to the soul.
Steady the breath,
strengthen the intention,
ask another question.
Not,
אֵיכָה *Eichah*,
How??
How did this happen?
Instead,
אֵיכָה *Eichah*,
How will I respond?

With praise and thanks,
with singing and chanting:

You, O God, and Your universe are unshaken,
and I, in this month of Av,
I am stirred in my soul.

Psalm 104 for Rosh Chodesh, the new month, begins on page 110.

with each psalm on its day.

Rosh Chodesh Elul   *Psalm 104:33*

Sing and Chant

אָשִׁירָה לַיְיָ בְּחַיָּי
אֲזַמְּרָה לֵאלֹהַי בְּעוֹדִי:

Let me sing to Adonai during my lifetime,
Let me sing praise to God while I still am!

Psalm 27:6:

וְעַתָּה יָרוּם רֹאשִׁי עַל אֹיְבַי סְבִיבוֹתַי וְאֶזְבְּחָה
בְאָהֳלוֹ זִבְחֵי תְרוּעָה אָשִׁירָה וַאֲזַמְּרָה לַיְיָ:

Now my head rises high above my enemies roundabout,
And in Your tent I'll offer offerings to the sound of t'ruah.
I shall sing and chant praises to Adonai!

The Elul moon rises,
the final month before the new moon of the New Year.
In my right pocket, a scrap of paper,
a simple citation, Psalm 104.
A whisper of assurance in the face of failure,
the world was made for me.
In the left pocket, its partner, Psalm 27.
A reminder in my success,
I am but dust and ashes.

In strength or weakness,
with confidence or self-doubt,
I sing and chant gratitude to God,
religiously and rigorously.

The monthly musical score for Psalm 104 is expansive:
I will sing to Adonai as long as I live,
all my life I will chant hymns to my God.
I raise my voice
and see with mind and heart:
infinite stretches of heavens,

... to remember, to thank, to praise

eternal foundations of earth,
endless varieties of species,
abiding cycles of seasons, sun, and stars.
I praise the God of My Creation.

In Elul the musical response of Psalm 27 is imperative.
I will sing and I will chant [NOW].

I sing.
My words cannot
call light into being,
bring life to animals,
or paint a green rainbow with grass across a marsh.
They can articulate my power in God's world:
to name, heal, speak truth,
to bless.

I chant.
Words are not necessary.
Humming vibrates the lungs
and each breath is like The First,
shimmering with shining Light
over the face of the deep,
onto my face,
into the depths of my being.

I reach into one pocket
to sing a litany of sins from A to Z.
I reach into the other pocket
to chant a wordless melody.
Notes spin
out among the stars
and wiggle into hidden crevices of memory.
In Elul, I will sing, and I will chant,
with gratitude,
on the way to a new year.

Psalm 104 for Rosh Chodesh, the new month, begins on page 110.

with each psalm on its day.

Acknowledgments

בְּיוֹם קָרָאתִי וַתַּעֲנֵנִי תַּרְהִבֵנִי בְנַפְשִׁי עֹז:
Daily I call out
and You, all of you,
are there,
inspiring me anew each day.

אוֹדְךָ בְּכָל־לִבִּי
I give thanks, with all my heart to:

The students of my Temple Emanu-El 9:00 a.m. central Zoom class-room, participating weekly from Dallas and places far beyond, with cameras on and hearts open, from August 2020 through January 2022, for creating a place for nourishment in a twenty-first-century pandemic with ancient psalms. Your faces, honesty, and life stories shaped this book and continue to nurture me.

An extraordinary village of friends who bless my life:
Connie Dufner, for her gracious prompts and perfect pens, which made this book better.
Rabbi Andrea L. Weiss, PhD, for her personal friendship and her professional words that amplify this practice.
Meredith Pryzant, for her gentle encouragement to continue this heart-opening work.

Fran Patterson and the Broadway Baptist Church of Fort Worth, for welcoming me to the Quiet House and reintroducing me to the possibilities of Isaiah 40:31. The 365 Homeowners Association, which continues to share with me a sacred space where psalms sing each day.

Rabbi Josh Warshawsky for his inspiring interpretation of the *Yotzeir Or* prayer. Rabbi Jonathan Slater, for his help chasing down a variety of sources. The staff team at CCAR, led by Rabbi Hara Person, and the CCAR Press—Chiara Ricisak, Raquel Fairweather-Gallie, Deborah Smilow, Debra Hirsch Corman, Michelle Kwitkin, and Scott-Martin

Kosofsky—led by Rafael Chaiken, director of CCAR Press, who with patience made this project a reality. Deep gratitude to Ariel Tovlev, 2021–23 CCAR Press intern, for their depth of perspective; Rabbi Jan Katz, CCAR Press editor 2021–22; and Rabbi Anne Villarreal-Belford, who brought her editorial gifts to the pages.

My colleagues and congregants, friends, at Temple Emanu-El in Dallas, for creating space for me to pursue my passion for psalms; and Jennifer Dietz, my administrative assistant, the calendar guardian of each day.

My parents, of blessed memory, whose voices and values live in me. My extended family, for their interest in the words and work that fill my days.

My immediate family, Larry (always at my side), Sam (only a text away), and Baskin Robbins (who was constantly at my feet); each one reminding me a hard dark day is only a day and a new one awaits with each dawn.

בֶּגֶד אֱלֹהִים אֲזַמְּרֶךָּ:
... in the presence of all Holinesses, I offer my voice.

—DEBRA J. ROBBINS
Wellfleet, Massachusetts

Notes

FOREWORD

1. Rachel R. Adler, "Two Psalms for Hard Times You Won't Find in Your Prayerbook," *Scriptions: Jewish Thoughts and Responses to COVID-19* (blog), Hebrew Union College–Jewish Institute of Religion https://scriptions.huc. edu/scriptions/two-psalms-for-hard-times-you-wont-find-in-your-prayer-book.

INTRODUCTION AND INVITATION

1. The entirety of this poem by Lea Goldberg (1911–70) can be found in *Mishkan T'filah: A Reform Siddur* (New York: Central Conference of American Rabbis, 2007), p. 145, adapted. Thanks to Rabbi Jonathan Slater for identifying the original publication in *Barak Baboker*, as part of a three-part collection *Shirei Sof HaDerech*, published around 1955. This poem has been set to music by Cantor Benjie Ellen Schiller.
2. "Months of the Jewish Year," My Jewish Learning, https://www.myjewishlearning.com/article/months-of-the-jewish-year/.
3. See the story of the Golden Calf in Exodus 32 and Rabbinic commentaries related to women refusing to participate in the pagan practice.
4. *Shulchan Aruch, Orach Chayim* 423. For additional details, see Isaac Klein, *A Guide to Jewish Religious Practice* (New York: Jewish Theological Seminary of America, 1979), p. 264.
5. Babylonian Talmud *M'gillah* 17b commenting on the *Sh'ma* (Deuteronomy 6:4).
6. Eliezer Ben-Yehuda (1858–1922) is credited with reviving the Hebrew language for use in schools and at home in Palestine and eventually in the State of Israel. See Jack Fellman, "Eliezer Ben-Yehuda and the Revival of Hebrew," Jewish Virtual Library, https://www.jewishvirtuallibrary.org/eliezer-ben-yehuda-and-the-revival-of-hebrew.
7. The psalms for *Kabbalat Shabbat* include Psalms 95–99, 29, 92, and 93.
8. The *minhag* (custom) is quoted in the back of *Tehillim Ohel Yosef Yitzchak* (Brooklyn: Kehot Publication Society, 2011) on p. 214: "It's known that the Alter Rebbe received the teaching from the Baal Shem Tov." Thanks to Rabbi Jan Katz at the CCAR for helping to locate the source.
9. Babylonian Talmud, *Chulin* 91b. Translation adapted from the William Davidson Talmud (Koren/Steinsaltz) found on Sefaria.
10. For more on *tamid* as psalms in the Temple, see I Chronicles 16:6, 37; for

details on the *tamid* lamp of the *Mishkan*, see Leviticus 24:1-4.

11. The Mishnah is a second-century code of law for Jewish life compiled by Rabbi Y'hudah HaNasi.

12. *Mishnah Tamid* 7:4.

13. The Talmud includes the text of the Mishnah and the Gemara (the legal and narrative materials that helped to explicate the text at the times it was compiled). The Jerusalem Talmud (from Israel) includes material from 200–500 CE, and the larger and more popular Babylonian Talmud includes materials from 200–600 CE. Both texts have also expanded over the generations to include commentaries from around the Diaspora.

14. Babylonian Talmud, *Rosh HaShanah* 31a.

15. Babylonian Talmud, *Rosh HaShanah* 31a.

16. *Biurei HaGra* on *Tamid* 7:4, cited by Raymond Apple, "The Psalms of the Day," *Jewish Bible Quarterly* 42, no. 2 (2014): 114–20.

17. This idea of seven historical periods that culminate in an ultimate Shabbat is first described within the *Zohar*, in *Sifra DiTz'niuta*. See Daniel C. Matt, "*Sifra di-Tsni'uta*, The Book of Concealment," in *The Zohar*, Pritzker Edition, vol. 5 (Stanford, CA: Stanford University Press, 2009), 2:176b, note 1, pp. 549–50. Tremendous thanks to Rabbi Jonathan Slater for chasing down the original source of this idea.

18. Rabbi Lord Jonathan Sacks, *The Koren Siddur*, Lobel Edition (Jerusalem: Koren, 2009), pp. 185–86.

19. *Kol Haneshamah: Daily* (Elkins Park, PA: Reconstructionist Press, 2006), p. 177 (attributed to Rabbi Hershel Matt).

20. Translation of Isaiah 66:22-23 adapted from Robert Alter, *The Hebrew Bible: A Translation with Commentary*, vol. 2 (New York: W. W. Norton, 2019), p. 846.

21. Psalm 104:19.

22. *Sof'rim* 19:9. This material was compiled around 750 CE.

23. The *Shulchan Aruch* by Joseph Karo (1563) is identified by Rabbi Isaac Klein in *The Guide to Jewish Practice* (New York: Ktav Publishing House, 1979) as the oldest source for this ritual; see *Shulchan Aruch*, *Orach Chayim* 423:3 for discussion of the Torah reading on Rosh Chodesh. *P'ninei Halachah*, *Haz'manim* 1:14:6 by Rabbi Eliezer Melamed (Jerusalem: Har Bracha Publications, 2005) affirms this practice.

24. Psalm 104:33, adapted from the Jewish Publication Society translation.

25. Elliott Holt, "Rereading Poems," *New York Times Magazine*, August 22, 2021, https://www.nytimes.com/2021/08/17/magazine/poetry-repetition.html.

26. Holt, "Rereading Poems."

27. Susan Cain, *Bittersweet: How Sorrow and Longing Make Us Whole* (New York:

Crown, 2022), pp. 148–50.

28. John Steinbeck, quoted in Maria Popova, "How Steinbeck Used the Diary as a Tool of Self Discipline, a Hedge against Self-Doubt, and a Pacemaker for the Heartbeat of Creative Work," *The Marginalian*, March 2, 2015, https://www.themarginalian.org/2015/03/02/john-steinbeck-working-days/.

29. Naomi Shihab Nye, "Always Bring a Pencil," in *Everything Comes Next: Collected & New Poems* (New York: Greenwillow Books, 2020), p. 22.

30. Billy Collins, "Advice to Writers," in *Sailing Around the Room* (New York: Random House, 2001), p. 8.

31. Babylonian Talmud, *Shabbat* 153a.

32. From the weekday *Amidah*, *Mishkan T'filah*, 84.

33. *Vayikra Rabbah* 9:7.

34. Psalm 100:4.

35. *Mishnah Rosh HaShanah* 1:1.

36. Richard Levy, *Songs Ascending: The Book of Psalms* (New York: CCAR Press, 2017).

TOOLS FOR PRACTICE

1. Wendell Berry, "How to Be a Poet (to remind myself)," in *Given* (Washington, DC: Shoemaker Hoard, 2005), p. 18.

DAILY DIRECTIONS

The practice for *Shir Shel Yom* was introduced in *Opening Your Heart with Psalm 27* and is revised here, with gratitude for the experiences and suggestions of the adult learners of Temple Emanu-El, Dallas, Texas.

SHIR SHEL YOM BLESSING

The opening words of this blessing and the closing formula for counting the days has its origins in the ritual of Counting the Omer.

Of the universe: Adapted from I Chronicles 16:23.

L'hazkir, ulhodot, ulhaleil: Adapted from I Chronicles 16:4.

On its day: Adapted from I Chronicles 16:37.

Blessed are You, Adonai: Adapted from I Chronicles 16:36.

Hallelu-Yah: This translation offers another name for God, Yah, resulting in hallelujah.

REFLECTIONS FOR FOCUS: INTRODUCTIONS TO SHIR SHEL YOM PSALMS
MOSHE CHAIM EPHRAIM OF SUDILKOV

Adapted from *Degel Machaneh Ephraim, Eikev*.

INTRODUCTION TO SUNDAY, PSALM 24

Note: The Hebrew language is built around a system of root letters, and the
 following key words, in varied grammatical forms, are all found in Psalm 24
 as well as the other Psalms of the Day.

Dor: Generation; Psalms 24:6, 48:14 (for Monday).

Tzedek: Justice; Psalms 24:5, 82:3 (for Tuesday).

Nefesh: Breath/soul; Psalms 24:4, 94:17, 19 (for Wednesday).

Lev: Heart; Psalms 24:4, 81:12 (for Thursday).

Kodesh: Holiness; Psalms 24:3, 93:5 (for Friday).

Adonai: God; Psalm 24:1 and Psalm 92:2,5,6,9,10,14,16 (for Shabbat/
 Saturday).

…the mundane power of my hands…: Deuteronomy 8:17-18.

In seven verses, Adonai: Psalm 92, vv. 2, 5–6, 9–10, 14, 16.

INTRODUCTION TO MONDAY, PSALM 48

Always begin with gratitude: Thanks to my beloved teacher of body and soul, Ruth
 Lurie.

Chesed: Psalm 48:10.

Six verbs in two verses: Psalm 48:13–14.

Pasgu. Scale the Heights: This is the only place in the Bible this word is used (a
 hapax legomenon), making it an invitation to consider something totally
 unique, a weekly opportunity not to be squandered.

This is a day that God has made: Psalm 118:24.

INTRODUCTION TO TUESDAY, PSALM 82

Dating back to Mishnah: Mishnah Tamid 7:4.

Clean hands and pure hearts: Psalm 24:4.

Women rejoicing: Psalm 48:12.

Come, let's sing: Psalm 95:1.

Calling us to account: Psalm 81:4.

Forever and a day: Psalm 93:5.

Children of the Most High: Psalm 82:6.

INTRODUCTION TO WEDNESDAY, PSALMS 94:1–95:3

Note: Because Psalm 94 ends on a negative note, the custom developed in some
 communities to include the opening three verses of Psalm 95, to conclude
 with thanks and praise.

On Wednesday our God is: All these names of God are derived from Psalms
 94:1–95:3.

INTRODUCTION TO THURSDAY, PSALM 81

Our Rock and our Redeemer: Psalm 19:15.

INTRODUCTION TO FRIDAY, PSALM 93
The tottering world of the week: Psalm 82:5 (for Thursday).

INTRODUCTION TO SHABBAT/SATURDAY, PSALM 92
Levites sang: I Chronicles 16:4–6.
The Talmud affirms: Babylonian Talmud, *Rosh HaShanah* 31a.
Double portions of wilderness manna: Exodus 16:22–23.
A second soul: Babylonian Talmud, *Beitzah* 16a.
Tell of Loving Connections: Thanks to my teachers at IJS for the Omer Reflections, Week 1 2022, which used this as a definition for *chesed*.
"You are on high forever, Adonai": Psalm 92:9, in Richard N. Levy, *Songs Ascending: The Book of Psalms; A New Translation* (New York: CCAR Press, 2017), p. 355.

REFLECTIONS FOR FOCUS: WEEK 1
RABBI YOSEI BAR Y'HUDAH
Adapted from Rabbi Yonah of Gerondi, commentary on *Pirkei Avot* 4:20, Sefaria.

BLUE GLOVES
Note: Last time, the angel wore a red vest. See "The Goodness of God Looks Like . . ." in Debra J. Robbins, *Opening Your Heart with Psalm 27* (New York: CCAR Press, 2019), pp. 62–63.

PROPER POSTURE
Elohim nitzav: Psalm 82:1.
Dal . . . Elyon: Psalm 82:3–4.
B'nei Elyon kulchem: Psalm 82:6.
Lo yadu v'lo yavinu: Psalm 82:5.
Kumah Elohim: Psalm 82:8.

GOD OF VENGEANCE
Eye for an eye or a tooth for a tooth: Exodus 21:24.
To judge with justice . . . upright heart: Psalm 94:15–16.
"The judgments . . . rightness of justice": Levy, *Songs Ascending*, p. 363, note 15.

WEIGHT OFF MY SHOULDERS
Seivel: Psalm 81:7.
The burden remains: Levy, *Songs Ascending*, p. 311, note 7.

DRESS LIKE GOD
Note: Thanks to Jodi Nicole Robbins, who in teaching me about her passion, fashion, inspired me to read Psalm 93:1 differently and see the midrash in this style-ish way.

Rabbi Chanina: Rabbi Chanina (late first–early second century CE), also known as Chanina bar Chama, moved to Israel from Babylonia to study Torah with Rabbi Y'hudah HaNasi (who edited the Mishnah).

God wears: Midrash T'hillim 93:1, in *The Midrash on Psalms*, trans. William Braude (New Haven, CT: Yale University Press, 1959), pp. 124–25.

Holy One . . .wraps light as a garment: Psalm 104:1–2.

REFLECTIONS FOR FOCUS: WEEK 2
RABBI CHIYAH BAR ABBA
Adapted from Babylonian Talmud, *Eiruvin* 54a–54b.

CLEAN HANDS CARRY BLESSING
Baruch atah: The blessing for washing hands (adapted) is traditionally recited before eating a meal that includes bread. It originates in *Mishnah Yadayim,* and the Rabbis crafted the practice and the blessing by expanding on Exodus 40:30–32 and Leviticus 15:11.

GOD'S EAST WIND
Ezekiel's voice: Ezekiel 27:26.
Jonah: Jonah 4:8.
Pharaoh: Exodus 10:13.
Pushing the water: Exodus 14:21.
Moses and Miriam: Exodus 14:31.
Ruach Elohim . . . present at Creation: Genesis 1:2.

THE JUDGE
All of us are worthy of fair judgment: Leviticus 19:15.

USE YOUR GIFTS
Shaped from clay . . . breath of life: Genesis 2:7.
Image of God: Genesis 1:17.
She shares and discovers: Genesis 3:6.
They hear the presence: Genesis 3:8.

WHERE THUNDER HIDES
God is not in the earthquakes: I Kings 19:11–12.
Praise to You: CCAR Daily Blessing App.

FOREVER
Note: Olam in the Bible means "eternity" and later comes to mean "world."
From eternity You have existed: Psalm 93:2, Jewish Publication Society translation.
God's promise to Noah: Genesis 9:12.

As Isaiah reflects and remembers: Isaiah 63:9, 11–12.
El Olam: Genesis 21:33, Abraham's name for God.

IT'S YOUR BUSINESS TO MAKE BIRDS
As You told Adam and Eve: Genesis 2:15.
God, how did it ever come to you: Mary Oliver, "Cormorants" in *Thirst* (Boston: Beacon Press, 2006), p. 18.

REFLECTIONS FOR FOCUS: WEEK 3
RABBI SHMUEL BAR NACHMANI
Adapted from Babylonian Talmud, *Eiruvin* 54b.

RAISE A FLAG OF BLESSING
To count the people: Numbers 4:2.
Aaron and his children: The Hebrew letter *shin* represents one of God's feminine names, *Shechinah*. Using analogies, *Shir HaShirim Rabbah* 2:9 imagines the Divine Presence peeking through the cracks of the priest's fingers to spread Her sacred healing blessing of Light.
May the Divine's countenance: Numbers 6:25–26.
May you "live long and prosper": This gesture is adopted by Mr. Spock in *Star Trek* to convey the blessing "Live long and prosper"; see https://archive.org/ details/LeonardNimoy15Oct2013YiddishBookCenter.
Ancient priests: Leviticus 6.
The Gates to Holiness: Mishkan HaNefesh, vol. 2, *Yom Kippur* (New York: CCAR Press, 2015), p. 628–30.

MY TRANSLATION
We have meditated on Your covenantal love: Levy, *Songs Ascending,* p. 183.
We witnessed, O God, Your kindness: Robert Alter, *The Book of Psalms* (New York: W. W. Norton, 2007), p. 169.
We are awed speechless, Source of Life, by your kindness: Pamela Greenberg, *The Complete Psalms: The Book of Prayer Songs in a New Translation* (New York: Bloomsbury, 2010), p. 100.
We imagined Your mercy: Martin S. Cohen, *Our Haven and Our Strength: The Book of Psalms* (New York: Aviv Press, 2004), p. 151.
O God, we beseech Your loyalty: Mayer Gruber, *Rashi's Commentary on Psalms* (Philadelphia: Jewish Publication Society, 2004), p. 366.
We meditate upon Your faithful care: JPS Hebrew-English Tanakh (Philadelphia: Jewish Publication Society, 2000), p. 1469.
God's endless and gracious: Exodus 34:6–7.
The generous kindness of Naomi: Ruth 1:8.

FOUNDATIONS ARE TOTTERING

Y'hudah HaLevi was right: Y'hudah HaLevi, "Lord, Where Shall I Find You?," in
the Penguin Book of Verse, ed. and trans. T. Carmi (New York: Penguin Books,
1981), p. 338. Y'hudah HaLevi (1075–1141) lived and wrote secular and religious poem in Spain until he immigrated to Palestine in 1140. This poem is
included as *Yah ana*, "Where might I go," in *Mishkan T'filah: A Reform Siddur*
(New York: CCAR Press, 2007), p. 171, and set to music by Dan Nichols,
making it accessible and familiar to many Reform Jews in the twenty-first
century.

SOOTHE THE SOUL

A unique word in the Bible: This word appears only here and in Psalm 139:23. The
Brown-Driver-Briggs Dictionary associates it with the root letters *sin-ayin-pei*, as
in Job 4:13 and 20:2.

I am unbalanced: From the psalm read on Tuesdays: "They do not know, they do
not understand, in deep darkness they stumble to and fro—all the foundations of the earth are tottering" (Psalm 82:5).

OPEN YOUR MOUTH WIDE

No manna at dawn: Numbers 11:4–9.
Falling quails: Numbers 11:31–34.
Suddenly appearing well: Genesis 21:17–19.
Gushing stream: Numbers 20:9–11.
Open my lips: Psalm 51:17.
I sing and chant: Psalms 104:33, 27:6.
Broad-minded: Like Rahav in Joshua 2.
Expansive of heart: Isaiah 60:5.
Steady in my steps: II Samuel 22:37
Open and free: II Samuel 22:20.

THE GUARD

Robed: Psalm 93:1.
Present from a place higher: Psalm 93:2.
With a call: Psalm 93:5.
On watch: Psalm 93:5.

WICKED LIKE WEEDS

At the very center: The center of Psalm 92, verses 8–12, is not included in *Mishkan
T'filah*, the prayer book of the Reform Movement.

Wicked like weeds: Thanks to Rabbi Richard Levy for his commentary to Psalm
92:8.

REFLECTIONS FOR FOCUS: WEEK 4
SHMUEL
Adapted from Babylonian Talmud, *Chagigah* 14a.

HONOR AT THE GATE
With the Psalmist: On Yom Kippur, as the day concludes with the *N'ilah* service, we pray for all the gates of righteousness to open with a *piyut* (religious poem) written in the format of an acrostic.

MIRIAM'S STORY
Let b'not Y'hudah, the town of Judah, rejoice: Robert Alter writes that in the Bible often "in urban contexts, 'daughters' (*banot*) refers to the outlying townlets, and the city itself is sometimes called 'mother'" (Alter, *The Book of Psalms*, p. 170).
Comparing terror and trembling: Psalm 48:7.
Like b'not Tz'lofchad... Mahlah, Noah, Hoglah, Milcah, and Tirzah: Numbers 26:33, 27:1, 36:11; Joshua 17:3. Many women go unseen, unheard, and unnamed in the Bible, but not these five daughters of Zelophehad, who are named four times!
These daughters... with open eyes and open ears: Psalm 48:9.
Long before Maya Angelou: Maya Angelou, *Phenomenal Woman: Four Poems Celebrating Women* (New York: Random House, 1995), p. 3. Maya Angelou (1928–2014) was an American memoirist, poet, and civil rights activist.

STUBBORN HEARTS
This is not the hard heart...: Exodus 4:21, a stiff heart (from Hebrew root letters *chet, zayin,* and *kof*). Exodus 7:3, a hard heart (from Hebrew root letters *kof, shin,* and *hey*). Neither is the same word used here (from Hebrew root letters *shin, resh,* and *resh*).
It is not the broken heart...: Psalm 147:3, the broken heart (Hebrew root letters, *shin, bet, resh*).
This heart of determination...: Jeremiah 9:13. This is the heart of a person who has turned away from Adonai, not listened to God's voice, worshiping the idols of his or her or their generations.

CURTAINS FOR THE HOUSE
Hosts, of golden daffodils...: William Wordsworth, "I Wandered Lonely as a Cloud," *Poems in Two Volumes: 1807* (Washington, DC: Woodstock Books, 1997), Vol. 2, p. 49.
Stretching Light like a tent cloth...: Psalm 104:2.

IT'S EASY BEING GREEN

...fruit trees of all sorts...: Genesis 1:11.

...we too are nourished with rain... Deuteronomy 28:12.

ROSH CHODESH
RABBI MORDECHAI YOSEF

Adapted from *Mei HaShiloach* on Genesis 28:12, *Vayeitzei* 3.

ROSH CHODESH TISHREI: PRAYERS FOR THE PATH

In the seventh month . . . sound of the shofar: Leviticus 23:24; Psalm 81:4.

Trembling on a mountain . . . from the darkness there will be light: The imagery draws upon Psalm 104, vv. 8, 10, 19.

The tenth of Tishrei: Leviticus 23:27.

Give thanks for resurrecting Breath: Rashi on Psalm 104:30 based on *Midrash T'hillim* 104:24.

My sins be cast away . . . and compassion reign: The imagery draws upon Psalm 104:35.

Sukkot is under the full moon Leviticus 23:34.

Human harvest, human faces: The imagery draws upon Psalm 104:14–15.

Shaped from . . . earth: Genesis 2:7.

Raising the fallen sukkah: Amos 9:11.

Shelter of peace: From *Hashkiveinu* prayer, "Spread over us a shelter of Your peace."

Sh'mini Atzeret–Simchat Torah: Leviticus 23:36.

Back to the beginning, b'reishit bara Elohim: Genesis 1:1.

I pray with the Psalmist . . . satisfied with what I've gathered: Psalm 104:33, 104:28.

Hallelujah: Psalm 104:35.

ROSH CHODESH CHESHVAN: SIMPLE AND SWEET

Sigd arrives: Sigd is an Ethiopian Jewish festival celebrated fifty days after Yom Kippur marking the covenant with God and has been a national holiday in the State of Israel since 2008. See "What is Sigd?" on *My Jewish Learning* (https://www.myjewishlearning.com/article/what-is-sigd/) for more details.

On the seventh day of this month we pray: Mishnah Taanit 1:3. "Grant rain and dew as a blessing" is the phrase added to the *Birkat HaShanim* blessing of the *Amidah*, beginning on the seventh of Cheshvan in Israel and on December 5 in the Diaspora, until Pesach. During the balance of the year, only the phrase "grant blessing" is added to the prayer. Details for this practice appear in many siddurim.

ROSH CHODESH KISLEV: A MESSAGE IN EACH LIGHT

Not to use them, only to behold them: Babylonian Talmud, *Shabbat* 21b. This phrase also appears in the prayer *Haneirot Halalu*, read each night of Chanukah.

Each angel of fire delivers a unique gift: Midrash T'hillim 104:7, 104:3 as found in *The Midrash of Psalms*, translated by William G. Braude (New Haven, CT: Yale University Press, 1959).

ROSH CHODESH TEVET: HIDDEN HOPE

And it's in Adar II: Mishnah M'gillah 1:4.

Eat no leavened bread: Leviticus 23:6.

Dwell in booths: Leviticus 23:42.

You hide Your face and I am terrified: Psalm 30:8.

Ramah and rom'mu: Psalm 30:2, *aromimcha,* "I will raise You up!"

Rinah: Psalm 30:6, *v'laboker rinah,* "But in the morning—song!"

Ratzon: Psalm 30:6, *birtzono,* "a lifetime of Your favor"; Psalm 30:8, *birtzon'cha,* "it pleased you."

Ruach: Psalm 104, v. 3, "wind"; v. 4, *ruchot,* "winds"; v. 29, *rucham,* "their breath"; v. 30, *ruchacha,* "Your breath."

R'fuah: Psalm 30:3, *vatirpa-eini,* "You healed me!"

ROSH CHODESH SH'VAT: HOLY WAYS

Fir and cypress: Commentators are divided about the identification of this tree. The *Brown-Driver-Briggs Dictionary* offers both.

Ever since the third day of Creation: Genesis 1:12.

Atikah—the Ancient One of Old: Thanks to Dr. Melila Hellner-Eshed for introducing me to this name of God from the *Zohar* based on Daniel 7:9, 13, 22.

I'm here to help: My gratitude to Richard Powers and his book *Overstory*, based on the work of Suzanne Simard, which I read in 2018. Their science and their creativity have transformed the way I encounter every tree.

The trees, the trees, just holding on: Mary Oliver, "The Trees," in *Evidence* (Boston: Beacon Press, 2009), p. 68.

ROSH CHODESH ADAR: THE MOON SMILES

"Whoever enters Adar increases in joy": Babylonian Talmud, *Taanit* 29a.

The moon marks this season: Psalm 104:19.

On the fourteenth day of the month: Esther 9:19.

As surely as birds make their nests: Psalm 104:17.

And springs flow downhill: Psalm 104:10.

The gladness, happiness, and honor that fills homes: Esther 8:16.

God rejoices: Psalm 104:31.

ROSH CHODESH NISAN: YOUR MESSENGER

Turned the sea into dry ground: Exodus 14:21.

Miriam was there: Exodus 15:20–21.

She knew . . . there would be reason to celebrate: M'chilta, Shirata 10, as cited by Claudia Setzer, in *The Torah: A Women's Commentary,* ed. Tamara Cohn Eskenazi and Andrea L. Weiss (New York: URJ Press and Women of Reform Judaism, 2008), p. 401.

ROSH CHODESH IYAR: STREAMS OF HEALING

In Marah, the Bitter Place: Exodus 15:23–25.

They are words of promise: Exodus 15:26 (the final four words), "I *Adonai* am your healer."

Mikveih Yisrael, Hope of Israel . . . Waters: Jeremiah 17:13.

Heal me, Adonai, *let me be healed:* Jeremiah 17:14.

ROSH CHODESH SIVAN: KNEAD WORDS OF TORAH

Note: The language of slave and master have become problematic in twenty-first-century America as we reckon with the historical enslavement of people in our country. The biblical narrative of the Jewish people tells the story of our enslavement, our redemption, and our transformation to free people through the gift of Torah; it maintains the language of slavery.

At Sinai after forty-nine days: Leviticus 23:15–16.

Choose life and blessing: Deuteronomy 30:19.

We are always numbering our days: Psalm 90:12.

ROSH CHODESH TAMMUZ: ME AND MY SHADOW

Like Joshua: Joshua 10:12–15.

Like Betzalel: Exodus 31:1–5.

Praised are You . . . You renew each day: Excerpted and adapted from *Yotzeir Or* prayer, in *Mishkan T'filah,* p. 228.

ROSH CHODESH AV: UNSHAKEN BUT STIRRED

Note: I am grateful to Rabbi Harold Kushner, one of the rabbis of my childhood, whose theology guided my father when the world around him was shaken and who steadied our family (and me) through many challenges.

Av is a month for remembering: Psalm 137:1. This psalm is traditionally read on Tishah B'Av, the ritual observance of the Ninth of Av.

Someplace in the Sinai wilderness: Numbers 14:11.

I know the ancient lament: Based on Lamentations 2:11.

Eichah: This same word appears in Lamentations 1:1, 2:1, and 4:1. The book is traditionally read/chanted on Tishah B'Av.

The mountains may tremble: Isaiah 54:10, fifth haftarah of consolation (for
parashat Ki Teitzei). This Torah portion is not read in Av but is part of a trajectory of healing and hope that begins in Av and continues through Elul leading
into Rosh HaShanah.

The words rouse me to turn: Lamentations 5:21.

ROSH CHODESH ELUL: SING AND CHANT

Note: Explore Psalm 27 and engage in the practice of reading it during the
month of Elul with *Opening Your Heart with Psalm 27*, written by the author,
published by CCAR Press.

I am but dust and ashes: Attributed to Rabbi Simcha Bunim, a great Chasidic master at the turn of the nineteenth century (Martin Buber, *Tales of the Hasidim:
The Later Masters* [New York: Schocken Books, 1969], pp. 249–50).

I will sing to Adonai as long as I live: Jewish Publication Society translation of
Psalm 104:33.

ACKNOWLEDGEMENTS

Daily I call out: Psalm 138:3.

I give thanks . . . in the presence of all holinesses: Psalm 138:1.

The translation of *Yotzeir Or* found in the epigraph is by Rabbi Josh Warshawsky;
his musical setting of this passage can be found at https://joshwarshawsky.
com/hameirah.

The Psalms used to surround the decorative pages are as follows:

Page 5, "Introduction to the Psalms": Psalm 24:1–10.

Page 22, "Shir Shel Yom Psalms": Psalm 48:1–12a.

Page 43, "Reflections for Focus: Shir Shel Yom Psalms": Psalm 82:1–8, Psalm
94:1–4a.

Page 45, "Week 1": Psalm 94:4b–16.

Page 59, "Week 2": Psalm 81:1–11.

Page 77, "Week 3": Psalm 95:1–5, repeated.

Page 93, "Week 4": Psalm 92:1–12.

Page 109, "Rosh Chodesh": Psalm 104:1–11.

Resources for Reading Psalms

Alter, Robert. *The Book of Psalms*. New York: W. W. Norton, 2007.
Translation and commentary that focus on the nuances of Hebrew language, metaphor, and historical context.

Baumol, Avi. *The Poetry of Prayer: Tehillim in Tefillah*. Jerusalem: Gefen, 2009.
Accessible chapters on various psalms of the prayer book, with citations for primary sources. Section 3 addresses each Psalm of the Day individually.

Braude, William G. *The Midrash on Psalms*. New Haven, CT: Yale University Press, 1959.
Translation of the ancient Hebrew text that captures Rabbinic interpretations and sermonic associations for all of the psalms.

Cohen, Abraham. *The Psalms*. London: Soncino Press, 1945.
Hebrew text, translation, introductory material, and curated verse-by-verse commentary from classical medieval commentators.

Cohen, Martin S. *Our Haven and Our Strength*. New York: Aviv Press, 2004.
Hebrew text, translation, and commentary in the form of a short essay connecting a theme of the psalm to the life of the reader.

Dahood, Mitchell. *The Anchor Bible on Psalms*. New York: Doubleday, 1965.
Academic commentary with linguistic, historical, and inter-biblical references.

Feld, Edward. *Joy, Despair, and Hope: Reading Psalms*. Eugene, OR: Cascade Books, 2013.
Short personal essays on faith focusing on fourteen different psalms, including *Shir Shel Yom* Psalms 82 and 92.

Fischer, Norman. *Opening to You: Zen-Inspired Translation of the Psalms*. New York: Penguin Compass, 2003.
A selection of psalms creatively translated reflecting Zen practices.

Glazer, Miriyam. *Psalms of the Jewish Liturgy: A Guide to Their Beauty, Power & Meaning*. New York: Aviv Press, 2009.
Translations and short essays on each Psalm of the Day, along with chapters on other psalms.

Greenberg, Pamela. *The Complete Psalms: The Book of Prayer Songs in a New Translation.* New York: Bloomsbury, 2010.

Poetic, vibrant, and accessible translation through which the reader is invited to engage directly with God.

Gruber, Mayer I. *Rashi's Commentary on Psalms.* Philadelphia: Jewish Publication Society, 2004.

First English translation of the Book of Psalms with the eleventh-century commentary written by the biblical commentator Rashi. Detailed notes identify additional sources and references.

Hakham, Amos. *Psalms with the Jerusalem Commentary.* Koschitzky ed. Jerusalem: Mosad Harav Kook, 2003.

Hebrew text and translation with extensive introduction and commentary as well as short theologically grounding essays.

Kol Haneshamah, Daily Edition. Elkins Park, PA: Reconstructionist Press, 2006.

Translations of *Shir Shel Yom* capture the diversity of the Holy One, and commentaries express a variety of contemporary theological perspectives.

Levy, Richard N. *Songs Ascending: The Books of Psalms; A New Translation.* New York: CCAR Press, 2017.

Hebrew text and translation with commentary that explores the nuances of the Hebrew and brief essays on the possible spiritual application of each psalm.

Mitchell, Stephen. *A Book of Psalms: Selected and Adapted from the Hebrew.* New York: Harper Perennial, 1994.

Fifty psalms are included in this modern, poetic, intimate collection.

Sacks, Jonathan. *The Koren Siddur.* Lobel Edition. Jerusalem: Koren, 2009.

Commentary to *Shir Shel Yom* psalms provides historical, spiritual, and practical insights.

Schachter-Shalomi, Zalman. *Psalms in a Translation for Praying.* Philadelphia: ALEPH, 2014.

Translation utilizing informal, personal language and terms to refer to God from the Renewal Movement of Judaism.

Segal, Benjamin J. *A New Psalm: The Psalms as Literature.* Jerusalem: Gefen, 2013.

Literary analysis of each psalm, with artistic renditions by David Sharir.

Steinberg, Paul. *Celebrating the Jewish Year: The Fall Holidays.* Philadelphia: Jewish Publication Society, 2007.

Excellent overview of Rosh Chodesh, the Jewish calendar as a spiritual cycle, and each holiday.

Appendix

TEN-YEAR CALENDAR FOR ROSH CHODESH

AS WITH MOST JEWISH HOLIDAYS, Rosh Chodesh begins at sundown the night before the date listed. This Jewish tradition comes from the story of Creation, about which the Torah writes, "There was evening and there was morning" (Genesis 1). Since evening is listed first, the "day" actually begins at sundown.

In addition, the Jewish calendar determines the lengths of each month by the cycles of the moon. While our secular calendar is based on the sun and has thirty to thirty-one days in a month, the Jewish calendar has twenty-nine to thirty days in a month. For months that have twenty-nine days, we observe only one day of Rosh Chodesh—on the first of the month. For months that have thirty days, we celebrate two days of Rosh Chodesh—on the thirtieth day of the previous month and on the first day of the next month.

Finally, the lunar calendar does not fully align with the solar calendar. While being only a couple of days short, over time this would cause the months to shift their places in our seasonal year. Since many of our holidays are tied to seasons (such as Sukkot occurring during the fall harvest and Passover taking place in the spring), the Jewish calendar had to be adjusted so that the lunar and solar calendars synchronized. To achieve this, the Rabbis created a "leap year" system to keep the holidays in their proper seasons. A non-leap year has one Adar, while a leap year has two—Adar I and II. There is a leap year in seven of every nineteen years. This explains why the dates of Jewish holidays change in our secular calendar from year to year, but they always appear during the same season.

Dates for 5784 (2023–2024) through 5793 (2033–2034) are included below. A perpetual calendar is available in the Reform Luach app from CCAR Press, which can be found in the Apple and Google app stores. Many Jewish calendars are also available online.

5784 (2023–2024)
Tishrei: September 16, 2023
Cheshvan: October 15–16, 2023
Kislev: November 14, 2023
Tevet: December 13, 2023
Sh'vat: January 11, 2024
Adar I: February 9–10, 2024
Adar II: March 10–11, 2024
Nisan: April 9, 2024
Iyar: May 8–9, 2024
Sivan: June 7, 2024
Tammuz: July 6–7, 2024
Av: August 5, 2024
Elul: September 3–4, 2024

5785 (2024–2025)
Tishrei: October 3, 2024
Cheshvan: November 1–2, 2024
Kislev: December 1–2, 2024
Tevet: December 31, 2024–
   January 1, 2025
Sh'vat: January 30, 2025
Adar: February 28–March 1,
2025
Nisan: March 30, 2025
Iyar: April 28–29, 2025
Sivan: May 28, 2025
Tammuz: June 26–27, 2025
Av: July 26, 2025
Elul: August 24–25, 2025

5786 (2025–2026)
Tishrei: September 23, 2025
Cheshvan: October 22–23, 2025
Kislev: November 21, 2025
Tevet: December 20–21, 2025
Sh'vat: January 19, 2026
Adar: February 17–18, 2026
Nisan: March 19, 2026
Iyar: April 17–18, 2026

Sivan: May 17, 2026
Tammuz: June 15–16, 2026
Av: July 15, 2026
Elul: August 13–14, 2026

5787 (2026–2027)
Tishrei: September 12, 2026
Cheshvan: October 11–12, 2026
Kislev: November 10–11, 2026
Tevet: December 10–11, 2026
Sh'vat: January 9, 2027
Adar I: February 7–8, 2027
Adar II: March 9–10, 2027
Nisan: April 8, 2027
Iyar: May 7–8, 2027
Sivan: June 6, 2027
Tammuz: July 5–6, 2027
Av: August 4, 2027
Elul: September 2–3, 2027

5788 (2027–2028)
Tishrei: October 2, 2027
Cheshvan: October 31–
   November 1, 2027
Kislev: November 30–
   December 1, 2027
Tevet: December 30–31, 2027
Sh'vat: January 29, 2028
Adar: February 27–28, 2028
Nisan: March 28, 2028
Iyar: April 26–27, 2028
Sivan: May 26, 2028
Tammuz: June 24–25, 2028
Av: July 24, 2028
Elul: August 22–23, 2028

5789 (2028–2029)
Tishrei: September 21, 2028
Cheshvan: October 20–21, 2028
Kislev: November 19, 2028

Tevet: December 18–19, 2028
Sh'vat: January 17, 2029
Adar: February 15–16, 2029
Nisan: March 17, 2029
Iyar: April 15–16, 2029
Sivan: May 15, 2029
Tammuz: June 13–14, 2029
Av: July 13, 2029
Elul: August 11–12, 2029

5790 (2029–2030)
Tishrei: September 10, 2029
Cheshvan: October 9–10, 2029
Kislev: November 8, 2029
Tevet: December 7, 2029
Sh'vat: January 5, 2030
Adar I: February 3–4, 2030
Adar II: March 5–6, 2030
Nisan: April 4, 2030
Iyar: May 3–4, 2030
Sivan: June 2, 2030
Tammuz: July 1–2, 2030
Av: July 31, 2030
Elul: August 29–30, 2030

5791 (2030–2031)
Tishrei: September 28, 2030
Cheshvan: October 27–28, 2030
Kislev: November 26–27, 2030
Tevet: December 26–27, 2030
Sh'vat: January 25, 2031
Adar: February 23–24. 2031
Nisan: March 25, 2031
Iyar: April 23–24, 2031
Sivan: May 23, 2031
Tammuz: June 21–22, 2031
Av: July 21, 2031
Elul: August 19–20, 2031

5792 (2031-2032)
Tishrei: September 18, 2031
Cheshvan: October 17–19, 2031
Kislev: November 16, 2031
Tevet: December 15–16, 2031
Sh'vat: January 14, 2032
Adar: February 12–13, 2032
Nisan: March 13, 2032
Iyar: April 11–12, 2032
Sivan: May 11, 2032
Tammuz: June 9–10, 2032
Av: July 9, 2032
Elul: August 7–8, 2032

5793 (2032–2033)
Tishrei: September 6, 2032
Cheshvan: October 5–6, 2032
Kislev: November 4, 2032
Tevet: December 3, 2032
Sh'vat: January 1, 2033
Adar I: January 30–31, 2033
Adar II: March 1–2, 2033
Nisan: March 31, 2033
Iyar: April 29–30, 2033
Sivan: May 29, 2033
Tammuz: June 27–28, 2033
Av: July 27, 2033
Elul: August 25–26, 2033

Index

Reflections for Focus by Day

About the Author

Rabbi Debra J. Robbins is a member of the clergy team at Temple Emanu-El in Dallas, Texas, focusing on teaching, pastoral care, and spiritual practice. She was ordained in 1991 at the Hebrew Union College–Jewish Institute of Religion, and is a graduate of the University of California at Berkeley and the Institute for Jewish Spirituality Clergy Leadership Program.

Rabbi Robbins has served the Central Conference of American Rabbis in a variety of leadership roles and is a member of the Women's Rabbinic Network. She was part of the City of Dallas Ethics Reform Task Force and served as president of Reading Village, a non-profit organization working in Guatemala to help teens become leaders through literacy. She is the cofounder of Common Table at the Fox and Crow, an organization founded in March 2020 to address food insecurity on the Outer Cape of Massachusetts. Rabbi Robbins is the current and founding chair of the Vaad HaMikvah of the Rabbinic Association of Greater Dallas in support of the Dallas Community Mikvah and is pursuing certification with the American Red Cross to do chaplaincy work in emergency situations.

In addition to contributing to multiple books, journals, and magazines, Rabbi Robbins is the author of *Opening Your Heart with Psalm 27: A Spiritual Practice for the Jewish New Year* (CCAR Press, 2019).

On a more personal note, Rabbi Robbins is married to Larry Robins, president and CEO of PediPlace in Lewisville, Texas. Her son, Sam, an avid mountain biker, lives and works in Denver, Colorado. She enjoys walking and training her Golden Retriever, treasures time reading (especially historical fiction), and loves relaxing by the tidal marsh in Wellfleet, Massachusetts.

www.ingramcontent.com/pod-product-compliance
Lightning Source LLC
Chambersburg PA
CBHW070329090426
42733CB00012B/2419